DESIRE AS PRAXIS

DESIRE AS PRAXIS

TOWARDS A QUEER SURREALISM

Peter Dubé

REBEL SATORI PRESS

New Orleans & New York

Published in the United States of America by
REBEL SATORI PRESS
www.rebelsatoripress.com

Cover art: *Le vol de l'aigle*, © Mathieu Beauséjour
Photo credit : Paul Litherland
Cover design by Sven Davisson

André Breton with his Collection, photo by Sabine Weiss, courtesy of Photo Elysée; *La rose noire* (The Black Rose), © Pierre Molinier, Adagp, Paris, 2024, courtesy the artist estate and Mennour, Paris; *Untitled*, double exposure photos by Peter Berlin courtesy of the artist and Clamp Gallery, NYC; still images from *Scorpio Rising*, Kenneth Anger, licensed through Alamy.

ISBN: 978-1-60864-354-7

For Mathieu with love.

"The greatest weakness in contemporary thought seems to me to reside in the extravagant reverence for what we know compared with what we do not yet know."
André Breton

ACKNOWLEDGEMENTS

To begin — deepest thanks to my pal Rebel Satori publisher Sven Davisson; I am profoundly grateful for your friendship, and unwavering support of my work. It means the world.

I also owe much gratitude to three individuals who oversaw this project in its earlier incarnation as a PhD dissertation: Jason Camlot, for his keen eye and mind, breadth of culture, perpetual good humour and editorial talents; Andre Furlani whose encyclopedic reading, wit, and ability to synthesize a vast range of material without any perceptible loss of detail or context were vital, and Thomas Waugh, a man whose intellectual rigour, knowledge of cinema (and queer history, politics, and culture more broadly), and nearly infallible judgement had an impossible to calculate impact. *Merci mille fois* to you all.

My thanks also go out to my friend and colleague Kate Sheckler whose careful reading and feedback were invaluable in shepherding this manuscript into its final book form.

Some of the material in Chapter 3 appears in a different context in my essay "Indexing Intimacies: The Affective Collections of André Breton and Samuel M. Steward" published in *Collection Thinking: Within and Without Libraries, Archives and Museums*, Camlot, Langford, Morra eds. Routledge, 2023.

Further, I send thanks to my wonderful network of queers, radicals, pleasure activists, arty gays, and most especially, members of the contemporary surrealist movement worldwide.

Your friendship and conversation remind me why I do this work: you folks rock.

Finally, to Mathieu Beauséjour, my beloved, my partner, my best friend and my ever-reliable accomplice in aesthetic outlawry, many thanks and much love. Let's keep doing this!

CONTENTS

FIGURES

CHAPTER 1
INTRODUCTION

Desire as Praxis; Towards a Queer Surrealism argues for a generative network of overlaps, intersections and shared concerns existing between surrealism and gay liberation. It proposes that these two traditions articulate related, and powerful, synthetic visions of the potential available to both human experience and the organization of the social. It points towards the possible synergies that might arise in considering them together and bringing their practices into alignment. It makes such claims despite André Breton's well-known homophobia, which the present writer has considered in other places[1], because its focus is on the movements' shared practices and ideas rather than on the personalities of individual members, however prominent. Furthermore, this work honours these commonalities without insisting on their identity, asking instead what they might learn from one another and what potential might lie in working through their practices simultaneously and tracing the many subtle lines of force tying them together and opening up the possibility of what I am imagining as a "Queer Surrealism." This is a potential, I will argue, whose investment in eros and affect holds ramifications for our conception of subjectivity,

1   Most notably in the introduction to the anthology *Madder Love.*

poetry, and the political alike.

Arising out of the ferment of the powerful modernist and leftist currents sweeping across Europe in the 1920s and 1930s, the Surrealist account of subjectivity/identity is transformational, oppositional, and integrative, concerned with attempting to bring the various levels of the psyche into closer synthesis while transforming its relationship to the world. It sought, in Breton's words, to "transform the world" and "change life" as it is lived daily. In their efforts to do so, the original group would appropriate techniques from psychoanalysis such as the interpretation of dreams and automatic writing (for which they owe an equal debt to mediumism and its cultivation of trance states), publish startling texts about interior life and the pulsations of desire, develop and play intricate verbal and visual games, blur the lines between various forms of expression, indulge in sessions of cultivated trance states and aimless wandering through the city in search of the marvellous, issue fiery tracts decrying what had hitherto been the assumed foundations of the social, and painstakingly cobble together an alternative history or genealogy for their movement.

A couple of generations later, the early Gay Liberationists would develop an account of subjectivity that emerged from the ferment of the sixties counterculture and the politics of the New Left. From this model they would begin to transform traditional conceptions of masculinity and femininity, reimagine the family and the individual within it, explore forms of sexual activity long repressed and, as Foucault (*Sex, Power*, 384) has suggested, create new ones, and seek to transform the experience of the city by imagining and creating eroticized spaces in its blank zones, publishing startling accounts of hitherto unspoken experiences of selfhood and painstakingly erecting an alternative history or genealogy of the emergence of a movement and its place in the world.

Thus, both movements postulate a new vision of subjectivity and new ways of being in the world simultaneously. This brings us to another programmatic similarity. In generic or formal terms, the articulation of a shared vision becomes a matter of the manifesto: a *formal statement of the programme* generated by that vision, and few groups have been more dedicated issuers of manifestoes than Surrealism and the proponents of Gay Liberation, among the earliest politically radical queers.

The proliferation of public statements by these political and intellectual groupings is a matter of historical record. The University of Michigan edition of André Breton's collected manifestoes includes no less than nine separate texts including the two *Manifestoes* themselves, the *Prolegomena to the Third Manifesto, The Political Position of Surrealism* and others. These tracts lay forth the animating vision of the movement, its fundamental aims and the strategies by which it seeks to achieve them. That volume, however, is far from an exhaustive selection of Surrealism's public declarations, nor are these the sole documents to lay out first principles. In a 1934 lecture in Belgium, for example, Breton makes this succinct declaration regarding the movement:

[W]e have attempted to present interior reality and exterior reality as two elements in process of unification, of finally becoming one. This final unification is the supreme aim of surrealism: interior reality and exterior reality being, in the present form of society, in contradiction (and in this contradiction we see the very cause of man's unhappiness, but also the source of his movement), we have assigned ourselves the task of confronting these two realities with one another on every possible occasion, of refusing to allow the pre-eminence of one over the other [...] (*What is Surrealism*, 116)[2]

Elsewhere, he states: "Surrealism [...] asserts our complete nonconformism clearly enough so that there can be no question of translating it, at the trial of the real world, as evidence for the defense. [...] Existence is elsewhere." (*Manifesto*, 47)[3]. Though these statements date from the early years of the movement and a generalized scholarly misapprehension has it that Surrealism ended with the death of André Breton, organized Surrealism in fact survives and thrives to the present day and has continued to issue public declarations about its work and goals uninterruptedly. Moreover, contemporary surrealists, Ronnie

2   "[N]ous avons tendu à donner la réalité intérieure et la réalité extéri-
eure comme deux éléments en puissance d'unification, en voie de *devenir commun*. Cette unification finale est le but suprême de l'activité surréaliste: la réalité intérieure et la réalité extérieure étant, dans la société actuelle, en contradiction – nous voyons dans une telle contradiction la cause même du malheur de l'homme mais nous y voyons aussi la source de son mouvement – nous nous sommes assigné pour tâche de mettre en toute occasion ces deux réalités en présence, de refuser en nous la prééminence à l'une sur l'autre [...]" (*Qu'est-ce que le surréalisme?*,11)
3   "Le surréalisme, tel que je l'envisage, déclare assez notre *non-conform-isme* absolu pour qu'il ne puisse être question de le traduire, au procès du monde réel, comme témoin à décharge [....] L'existence est ailleurs" (*Mani-feste*, 60)

Burk especially notably, have been equally involved in queer political formulations such as ACT UP, providing significant points of contact between the movements and demonstrating the extent to which some participants at least find intellectual and political value in the intersection.The 1997 anthology *The Forecast is HOT* collects "tracts and collective declarations" by the movement in the United States issued throughout the '60s and '70s while new Surrealist Journals such as *Hydrolith* (Berkeley) and *Phosphor* (Leeds, UK), which began publishing in the 21st century, publish declarations and other texts by organized Surrealist groups and individuals from around the world.

Though there is a tendency to view Gay Liberation as a purely political movement, even the briefest review of the key journals, *Gay Sunshine* and *Fag Rag* for example, will correct any such impression given the prominence of poetry in their pages and the attention given to more general discussions of literature. And the literature of the more radical tendencies of the gay liberation movement shows equal dedication to programmatic statements. From early in the movement's emergence one might read the following in Carl Wittman's now canonical (if too-often neglected) *Gay Manifesto* (1969-1970):

"We want to make ourselves clear: our first job is to free ourselves; that means clearing our heads of the garbage that's been poured into them. This article is an attempt at raising a number of issues and presenting some ideas to replace the old ones." (381)

A near-contemporary (1973) text offers this: "Our purpose is to urge all such men [...] to become traitors to the class of men by uniting in a movement [...] to change ourselves from non-masculinists into anti-masculinists" (Dansky et al, 436). In these affirmations we hear a call for social and psychic transformation not dissimilar to that of surrealism: a demand to transform the mind and the world, and for nonconformism (in gender presentationa, here, but other tracts have other, related, concerns such as family structures or romantic relationships). This dedication to the manifesto has continued among radical queers to the present day and become a recognized hallmark of the movement(s). As Juhasz and Ma have noted, "Queers love manifestoes. We love writing and reading them. From Sergei Eisenstein to Valerie Solanas to Chris Crocker, queers have crafted manifestoes [...] [it] is a fitting mode of expression for those who have been historically marginalized." (360). Significantly, this statement was made in 2013 and prefaced a selection of some fifteen new manifestoes by queer media radicals.

Having noted such related programmes and a shared investment in the manifesto as a formal articulation of programme, one is left with the question of why these particular collectivities were driven to reconsider and restate their intellectual and political positions with such regularity. Some possible factors are salient in a consideration of the thing itself, the manifesto: a form that, as it lays out guiding principles, is necessarily subject to perpetual revision in the face of new knowledge and changing situations. The word derives from the Latin word, *manifestus,* meaning to make visible or comprehensible, but the trace of the word *manus*, or hand, is present as well. From the level of etymology up, the manifesto is an action, a gesture. Thus any such text should do more than simply propose action; it should, in some way, constitute action. This understanding underlies Steven Marcus of Columbia University's characterization of the manifesto form as a kind of "action writing." It is this dynamism that gives the form such appeal to groups whose vision is not a mere question of understanding reality, but transforming it. Breton's *Manifesto*, for example, is a summons to a kind of epistemological insurrection, the true range of which he declared both in that text, and in his "Speech to the Congress of Writers" where he states bluntly: "'Transform the world,' Marx said; 'change life,' Rimbaud said. These two orders are one for us" (241).[4] In clearly related terms, Dansky *et al* agitate for a total transformation of traditional ideas of masculinity, which is to say a fundamental change in one of the basic categorical divisions of the social. But both these volatile utterances do not merely call for this or that action, they constitute actions in and of themselves; they are performative in a number of significant ways.

First, and most basically, the highly charged language and rhetorical posture of the manifesto as a form instruct readers in its reading or interpretation. As Mary Ann Caws has suggested, readers are directly subjected to an attempt to bring them into agreement with the manifesto's positions: "it wants to make a persuasive move from the 'I believe' of the speaker'

---

4   " 'Transformer le monde', a dit Marx; 'changer la vie', a dit Rimbaud: ces deux mots d'ordre pour nous n'en font qu'un" (*Discours*, 95).

toward the 'you' of the listener or reader" (xx). In this way, the manifesto form, as a text that articulates its concerns in the most deliberate and interpellating ways, creates "its own conditions for reception" (xxiii). The manifesto creates substantively new cognitive and experiential spaces, which points to the profound performativity associated with surrealist and gay liberation work, both textual and lived.

Moreover, all manifestoes, insofar as they attempt to articulate a position relative to a vision or goal, necessarily create an "us" and a "them," they divide the world into those who share the articulated vision – its partisans – and those who do not, whether they cleave to the status quo or to some other new vision. Such a rearrangement of the social is a speech act; it is an effect in the actual world. This is a characteristic of the genre *per se*, however the manifestoes here at issue take it further; they do not merely divide the social programmatically, they add to the order of the social in its very substance.

The manifestoes of surrealism and the queer radicals define new identities, new categories of people. With the issuance of the first *Manifesto of Surrealism* (a movement), the category "surrealist" (a kind of practice certainly, but also a kind of person — one involved in that practice) enters the world. Moreover, the surrealist is given a set of defining markers or properties: a concern with bringing together aspects of existence previously seen as irreconcilable, the practice of automatism and revolutionary fervour, for example. The early declarations of the queer liberation movements do similar work; they create the contemporary "out" gay man. Prior to these declarations, outside of the all-but-invisible gay underworld, there was no public notion of the gay man; in its place was the "homosexual," a category determined not by self-affirmation, but by medical and legal institutions, making it a social category in utter opposition to Wittman's and Dansky's (among others) call for liberation. Most importantly these are identities that are not conferred by birth, faith or culture, but are based in and require action. To be a surrealist is to practice automatism, to seek the magical "point of the mind" (Breton, *Second Manifesto*, 123)[5] at which binaries cease to have a hold, while to be a gay liberationist requires that one "come out," a deliberate strategy first articulated in such manifestoes and one that transforms the social (and quite possibly the economic and security) situation(s) of the one who elects to do so. An "out" gay man, after all, is as radical a transformation as that which saw the "sodomite," (that theological creature) become the homosexual at some point in the nineteenth century. Both these new identities require active engagement in political action and it is in the confluence of desire, action and public affirmation that one begins to first see the possible outline of a Queer Surrealism, another new vision; a vision in which the subject and the world are seen as, to borrow from Breton, "communicating vessels." In which they are seen in some ways, as even consubstantial, wound up in the same net of desire and transformed by it; a vision in which the familiar truism "the personal is political" takes on new, and strange, senses and forms.

And here might lie some initial explanation of the vehemence, and the frequency, of such public declarations. The issuance

5   "un certain point de l'esprit" (*Second manifeste*, 72)

of a manifesto is the first of the actions that might get us to this notion of a transformed world, or at least a transformed experience of it and its opportunities, spaces, and pleasures. Manifestoes are insistent in tone because the stakes are so large and the resistance so great. After all, as Quebec surrealist Mimi Parent once wrote, one must "Knock hard. Life is deaf" (cited in Rosemont, xxix)

SOME DEFINITIONS

In a work tracing the subtle lines of force and praxis animating two cultural tendencies with significant histories and contested senses, both of which share a conspicuous engagement with language, definition, and speech acts, it will be useful to take a moment at the beginning of the project to define two central terms. Therefore, the words "surrealism" (and its cognates) and "queer" (and its cognates and related terms) are used in the following way(s) in this work.

DEFINING "SURREALISM"

The present work takes "surrealism" (and its derivatives and cognates) in its broadest sense. As is generally the case, the word is meant here to designate the ideas and practices, public statements and other manifestations of the artists, writers and thinkers associated with the original Parisian group around Breton as well as those involved with other active and self-identified surrealist groups (such as those in Prague or London, for example, though by no means limited to those.) It also includes in its understanding of "surrealism" individuals active in the movement for a time, even if formally "expelled" at one point.[6] This work also recognizes as surrealist affiliated figures generally regarded as "dissidents" from the movement such as Georges Bataille and those in his orbit, and the various publications and groups with which he was involved (*Acéphale*, for example, and the *Collège de Sociologie*.) Though arguments have been made that Bataille and his circle are best understood as external to surrealism proper, the balance of evidence leans towards seeing the circle as part of a surrealist tendency writ large; certainly the writing of the two coteries is often in dialogue (and this from so early – and oppositional – a tract as *Un cadavre*) and individual persons travelled between the groups with regularity. There is a clear sense that, as Michael Richardson has observed, attempts to dissociate Bataille from the movement go against the author's own "affirmation of his fundamental solidarity with it, and his general agreement with the thinking of André Breton" (*Introduction*, 1). Indeed, any close reading of the published work makes it difficult not to note that "[t]aken as a whole, his early writings appear as an alternative realization of the surrealist impulse and, as such, invite a renewed understanding of the meaning of this movement" (Hewson and Coelen, 3). Moreover, Bataille acknowledges the fundamental relationship on numerous

6   Some figures often associated with surrealism in the popular imagination have, however, been deliberately excluded, notably Jean Cocteau. Though Cocteau shares some surrealist interests (dreams and mythology for example) with the figures included, his interest in and use of them tends to remain largely for their merely artistic or aesthetic potential, which places him, properly speaking, outside the purview of this work and its argument.

occasions, most notably when he writes of himself in 1946, well after the scuffles of the twenties and thirties, as surrealism's "old enemy from within" (*Subject of Slumbers*, 49).[7] This is a position he would reiterate and insist on; for example, he does so in his essay "The Surrealist Religion" of 1948, when he writes of surrealism's accomplishments using the inclusive "us" and asserts his continuing commitment in this way: "I believe one cannot insist too strongly on the necessity of binding consciousness to depersonalization. It seems to me that surrealism has gone a long way in this direction, but the way remains open, and it is necessary for us to penetrate further into it." (80).[8] Moreover, Bataille, would actively defend surrealism's continuing relevance against the attacks of the ascendant existentialists during the post-war period, going so far as to assert that *"in terms of mankind's interrogation of itself, there is surrealism and nothing"* (*Subject of Slumbers*, 51, italics in original).[9]

Finally, and despite the many attempts by scholars to define or impose a historical terminus for surrealism, whether it be World War 2 or Breton's death in 1966, this study includes as constituent of surrealism the work of the many writers and artists active in, influenced by, and acknowledging the influence of, the movement up to the present day and (presumably) beyond.

7   son vieil ennemi *du dedans*, que je suis," (*Assoupissements*, 31).
8   Je crois que l'on ne saurait trop insister sur cette nécessité de lier la conscience à la dépersonnalisation. Il me semble que le surréalisme s'est avancé profondément dans cette voie, il me semble aussi que cette voie demeure ouverte et qu'il nous est nécessaire de nous y enfoncer d'avantage." (*La religion surréaliste*, 393).
9   *"en matière d'arrachement de l'homme à lui-même*" il y a le surréalisme et rien" (*assoupisements*, 32).

Our understanding of surrealism in this work is as a body of ideas and practices regarding the nature of consciousness, desire, and the interpenetration of the subject and the world (both sensual and political) deployable by anyone and not necessarily tied to any particular historical or organizational situation.

DEFINING "QUEER"

The particular value and largest efficacy of the word "queer" arguably lies in its unfixed nature, the slipperiness of the various meanings attached to it. Such ambiguity has been present in the notion of the queer from its beginnings; even at the lexical level the word is riddled with complexity being at once an adjective, a verb, and a noun and having slightly different senses in each of those cases. Its use, therefore, requires greater than typical efforts to clarify, or explain its specific operations in particular texts. Such flexibility has no doubt aided in the process of its wide taking up within the academy, where scholars have argued that the term is a "political metaphor without fixed referent" and "[insisted] on queer studies' intellectual and political relevance to a wide field of social critique […] while realigning its political attentions, historical foci, and disciplinary accounts" (Eng *et al*, 1). This broadening of the notion of the queer and its deployment in so various a range of interventions highlights both the flexibility of the term and its perceived usefulness; however, it does beg a number of important questions: how does so amorphous a notion achieve theoretical coherence? What, in short, might it not apply to? Heather Love points to this emergent issue in "Queer Theory's Everything Problem" when she writes, "[w]hat makes queer gravitate to these points of intervention and not others? Why not, in fact, everything?" (175).

Although Love raises a pertinent question with significant theoretical import for the field of queer studies, it remains possible to identify some potential points of coherence in how the word queer has been deployed. Of particular interest to me in this project is the manner in which the "queer" often attempts to position itself in a productive interstice: as being both transgressive by nature (the queer as non-normative, taboo-shattering, eccentric) and unfixed or indeterminate (the queer as neither-nor, fluid, mutable). This ambiguity is constitutive of the very notion:

> Queer is by definition whatever is at odds with the normal, the legitimate, the dominant. There is nothing in particular to which it necessarily refers. It is an identity without an essence. 'Queer' then, demarcates not a positivity but a positionality vis-à-vis the normative (Halperin, 62).

Furthermore, despite the broadened uses made of the term in a range of disciplines, queer usually attaches itself specifically to transgressions of the normative in sexual behaviour or gender identity/presentation, and less often to other kinds of disallowed behaviours and ideas. A cross-dresssing sadomasochist, for example, will be denounced as "queer," but a council communist, however sanctioned politically, socially or otherwise, will not be so identified. Thus, without necessarily desiring to shut down "queer's inexhaustible definitional mobility" (Amin, 179) the word will be used in this narrower way here: in a way that recognizes that "little queer scholarship actually uses queer in an entirely dereferentialized manner," that most often "queer scholarship does in fact reference sex, gender, and sexuality" (179). The term will be used in examining a number of representations of queer sexuality and queer identity in these senses in my research. In particular, I will engage with texts (both literary and cinematic) that deal with the culture of cruising/public sex and BDSM activities. Such representations are valuable for my project because in both cases they act to destabilize "normative" understandings of such things as shared versus private space, public and counter-public, and even what constitute "sexual" acts themselves; all of which are fundamental social, cultural and political norms. This offers the further benefit of grounding my understanding of queer in praxis, in specific embodied contexts and situations, and such practice is foundational to my project here. Moreover, I will root my analysis in some of the earliest moments of gay liberation, moments in which it was closely associated with radical strains of the counter-culture, and trace the persistence of such strains through to the present day; in doing so I will set aside the more recent emergence of an "assimilationist" or "homonormative" ethos which is at odds with an oppositional position. This oppositionality to the normative will underpin my use of "queer" in its larger sense, when applied to situations, ideas and contexts rather than to persons or specific subjects. However, given how such practices often give rise to particular subject positions and communities, when denoting persons or particular queer sexual "subjects," however, I will use the word "queer" even more specifically; I will generally be referring to gay or bisexual men, to the wide range of men who have sex (of various sorts) with men. In some cases these men may also be members of other sorts of related constituencies (gender, racial and so on) but my focus will be on their same-sex desires and practices. The culture of homosexually active men is my focus here for a variety of reasons: such art and literature have long been a research interest of mine and are the corpora with which I am most familiar, and I find particularly fascinating resonances existing between them and the archives of surrealism. Further, I recognize the value of "own voices" in writing and publishing, and believe them to be of particular importance when discussing actual, embodied practices like those that are my subject here. And, as will be explored in Chapter 2, sex and desire are constituent of both movements and thus a focus on sexual identity and sexual behaviour could be the most generative approach in theorizing a "Queer Surrealism."

Finally, as meaningful research and exegesis require focus and depth and given how little has yet been done in the area, this work constitutes a starting point in some ways, so a narrower focus seems appropriate. Certainly, as this book's use of the indefinite article "a" (meaning one possibility of a queer surrealism) in its subtitle necessarily implies, similar work could be done with respect to lesbians, and other queer subjectivities, and I not only welcome it, but am sure to be among its readers if and when it appears.

DEFINING "GAY LIBERATION"

For the purposes of this project, "Gay Liberation" will be taken to refer to the political theories and ideas emerging during and just after the incidents of Stonewall in June 1969, which were informed by the ideas and programmes of the New Left and that led to the formation of the Gay Liberation Front.[10] These ideas conceived of Gay Liberation as profoundly entwined with feminist, anti-capitalist, anti-imperialist, and anti-racist politics rather than as a simple single-issue movement for the decriminalization and/or depathologization of homosexual acts. They were also less driven by identitarian approaches than contemporary gay politics and conceived of sexuality as a spectrum rather than a collection of defined orientations. The term will also be used to identify contemporary approaches that consciously attempt to preserve, advance and develop these ideas in the present day as can be found in the work of the Against Equality Collective, Gayle Rubin and many queer anarchist groups and writers. "Gay Liberation" is thus meant to suggest a political conception and/or programme that is invested in social transformation in the broadest sense rather than the acquisition of "rights" and "privileges" within the existing system.

DEFINING "DESIRE"

The word "desire" is used here in a sense closely tied to

---

10   Martin Duberman's *Has the Gay Movement Failed?* provides a succinct, clear account of the GLF's history, ideas and afterlives.

the psychoanalytic tradition and the Freudian notion of the "libido" as a form of "mental energy, with which processes, structures and object-representations are invested" and which has "a source, the body or the id," and "as being distributed between various structures or processes" (Rycroft, 95), which operates as the "dynamic manifestation of [the sexual instinct] in mental life" (Freud, cited in Laplanche and Pontalis, 239). Its use is also meant to suggest the sense of "wish" implicit in Freud's use of "wunsch" in the original German, and which is now usually rendered as "desire" in English. This positions desire more specifically, for Lacan in particular, as operating "in the rift which separates need and demand; it cannot be reduced to need since, by definition, it is not a relation to a real object independent of the subject but a reaction to phantasy" (Laplanche and Pontalis, 483), a phantasy that, for our purposes here could take the form of another person, some object or the elusive utopian horizon underlying the praxes of both surrealism and queerness. The term "eros" will also sometimes be used to denote this energy as well.

DEFINING THE FIELD

Given the programmatic impulse already noted at work in both surrealism and the "queer" it becomes necessary to interrogate the motivations underlying the programmes: what drives them; what are their goals and aims? What merits the attention and efforts of those participating in the surrealist movement and the movement for queer liberation?

Despite the passage of almost a century, and one that has

been particularly rich in artistic, social, and scholarly growth and ferment at that, surrealism continues to occupy a fraught, ambiguous position in intellectual history. The archive of critical writing provides an indication of just how uncertain this position actually is; even the briefest search will return studies whose titles make the variety of lenses through which this peculiarly slippery object continues to be viewed very clear. Such a search will, of course, find exegeses of surrealist visual art, cinema, and literature: arguments linking it to wildly divergent sorts of literary practices (Romantic and Objective poetry, the horror fiction of the Gothic novel and that of H.P. Lovecraft, the tradition of pornographic writing) but one will also find readings of the movement in terms of Marxist and anarchist politics (Gifford, Lewis), psychoanalysis (Lusty, Lomas), phenomenology and epistemology, (Hegarty, Kavky) decolonization of the Caribbean, Africa and other regions (Fijalkowski/Richardson, Ades, LeBrun), and, more recently, one finds studies of the movement in terms of crime (Eburne) or of hermeticism and magic (Bauduin). Given the range and extent of surrealist activity, the range of critical commentary seems reasonable, indeed less diversity could seem suspect. Though this variety certainly testifies to both the quantity and the precision of the critical attention brought to bear on the movement it also indicates something of the elusiveness of surrealism itself, its refusal, despite its multiple programmatic statements, to be easily classified – the refusal to specialize one notes in declarations like this:

We have nothing to do with literature; But we are quite

capable, when necessary, of making use of it like anyone else [...] *Surrealism* is not a new means of expression, or an easier one, nor even a metaphysic of poetry. It is a means of total liberation of the mind *and of all that resembles it.* (Breton *et al*, "Declaration", 240-241, emphasis in original).[11]

Here, and in other similar statements, the surrealist project *is* its ambitions – and those ambitions are vast: the desire to free not only the mind from its ordinary restraints but "everything that resembles it" as well, which – necessarily – can only be the object of the mind: the world as it is experienced. Moreover, statements such as this by Louis Aragon, demonstrate that such an expansive self-conception was both deliberate and determinant:

We have seen then what the Surreal is about. But to really understand the concept we have to extend it; view it perhaps like the horizon which continually flees before the walker, for like the horizon this concept exists between the mind and what it knows it will never reach. (*Wave of Dreams*, 23)[12]

11   Nous n'avons rien à voir avec la littérature; Mais nous sommes très capables, au besoin, de nous en servir comme tout le monde [...] Le *sur-réalisme* n'est pas un moyen d'expression nouveau ou plus facile, ni même une métaphysique de la poésie; Il est un moyen de libération totale de l'esprit *et de tout ce qui lui resemble*," ("Déclaration", 218-219)
12   On voit alors ce qu'est le surréel. Mais en saisir la notion ne peut se faire que par extension, au mieux c'est une notion qui fuit comme l'horizon devant le marcheur, car comme l'horizon elle est en rapport entre l'esprit et ce qu'il n'atteindra jamais," (*Une vague*,18).

In this passage, Aragon offers a clear description of the "surreal," necessarily the defining objective of a movement called "surrealism." It is a sort of utopian place or thing, a horizon that is aimed for by all surrealist activity but, paradoxically, it is a goal which he bluntly affirms one should never expect to achieve. Unsurprisingly, so broad an objective as surrealism's has led to a critical tendency to read specific manifestations of the movement very closely (hence the diversity of the archive), but to leave summative declarations more general. Michel Foucault, for example declared surrealism's purview to be the "domain of experience" (*Breton*, 12) while Maurice Blanchot spoke of it as " a pure practice of existence," (407). Though these readings reflect surrealism's avowed ambition to transform life and the world at once, they provide only the broadest framework for engaging with both the movement itself and the span of critical approaches to it.

Significantly for this work, a similar broadness of ambition can be discerned in the work of writers, artists and thinkers working in the field of LGBT studies and Queer Theory. In his germinal work *Cruising Utopia* José Esteban Muñoz writes of queerness thus:

> Queerness is not yet here. Queerness is an ideality. Put another way, we are not yet queer. We may never touch queerness, but we can feel it as the warm illumination of a horizon imbued with potentiality. We have never been queer, yet queerness exists as an ideality that can be distilled from the past and used to imagine a future. (1)

His suggestion that "queerness" acts as a horizon echoes, in ways both profound and generative, Aragon and Breton's quest for the "surreal." For Muñoz, queerness too is something to be envisioned, pursued or sought for, and it contains the possibility at least for radical transformations of subjectivity, lived experience and the social all at once. He addresses this radical potential directly in an interview with Lisa Duggan when he says "[t]his is the most generative moment in the utopian function. [...] It is the goal of enacting a world, the actual creation of that goal and the actual movement towards that goal" (*Hope and Hopelessness*, 279). Here Muñoz points to the significance of the ideality he identifies; it operates both as an endpoint and a basis for practice, and it is bluntly utopian. Thus, as such statements make clear – one from a prominent contemporary queer theorist and the other from one of the key first generation surrealists (and later Marxist poet and theorist) separated by the best part of a century – what ties their thought and strategies together is a shared focus on a foundational ideality. These are idealities that, though distinct from one another, share some very curious qualities or characteristics: each is a horizon, or endpoint, against which not only is reality measured, but against which it is experienced and one that one might not expect to ultimately reach. To that extent, both are models of an imagined utopia. And"utopia" is a word for a human-realized paradise whose very etymological roots (it derives from the ancient Greek words for "no place" or "nowhere") contain a suggestion of its own impossibility. If something is nowhere can it be said to exist? Moreover, to freight the term for the loftiest of human social and political aspirations with the spectre of its absence, its relentless deferral, is to create a signifier that can only be haunted: haunted by its own ephemerality, and how much else? The matter is made worse, of course, when we consider the history of actual attempts at utopia.

José Esteban Muñoz makes the point thus:

The history of actually realized utopian enclaves is, from a dominant perspective, a history of failures. Hope and disappointment operate within a dialectical tension in this notion of queer utopia. Queerness's failure is temporal and, from this perspective, potentially utopian, and inasmuch as it does not adhere to straight time, interrupting its protocols, it can be an avant-garde practice that interrupts the here and now. To perform such interruptions is not glorious or heroic work. (*Cruising Utopia*, 155).

This reflection of Muñoz's (like the one above) appears in a book rooted in a foundational insight regarding the impossibility of achieving actual "queerness" and its consequent immense value as a horizon, an ideality that can be extracted from the existent, and the past, for the imagining of the future. Building on Ernst Bloch's work, Muñoz draws the connections between queerness and utopia, asserting time and again the "not-yet-hereness" of the queer and the ways in which its perpetual deferral is the source of its inexhaustible potential and a sort of happy failure at same time. He insists "[q]ueerness and the politics of failure are linked insofar as they are about doing 'something else' " (154) and undoing the stranglehold of normativity in areas as far-ranging as the experience of time (think of the late start times of Jack Smith's performances) and the experience of sex (the curious intimacy and impersonality that operates in, for example, public cruising); both "queerness" and some version of "failure" are driven by a perpetual, and finally unsatisfiable, longing for possibility. Foregrounding the role of longing or desire, Muñoz states that "queerness is a structuring and educated mode of desiring that allows us to see and feel beyond the quagmire of the present" (1) and he stresses its performativity and its denaturalization (151). In this way, as a kind of desire queerness can and will push at limits and sometimes fail to satisfy, and in so doing provoke new efforts towards new objects: a dialectical process whose specificity Muñoz confronts head on.

Significantly enough Breton makes a similar concession regarding the utopian horizon that motors the political, philosophical and creative efforts of surrealism:

I believe in the future resolution of these two states, dream and reality, which are seemingly so contradictory, into a kind of absolute reality, a *surreality*, if one may so speak. It is in quest of this surreality that I am going, certain not to find it but too unmindful of my death not to calculate to some slight degree the joys of its possession.

(*Manifesto* 14)[13]

Thus these theorists/poets hold that neither of these idealities has ever actually been immediately experienced, nor have they any expectation that one will ever know it, and it is in that unknowability, at least partly, that its value is understood to be. The horizon allows for perennial reconsideration, perennial hope, and perennially new pleasures.

Importantly, this frank sidelining of the question of achievability places the whole value of the horizon in its pursuit; in its constituting an object of desire. This is entirely consistent in the case of these two, for lack of a better word, movements, both of which are particularly concerned with the domain of the erotic; as we see here, both "queerness" (however that is construed) and the "surreal" are in Buñuel's words "obscure objects of desire," which we pursue without necessarily ever achieving, or even expecting to achieve. This ideality, constantly pursued and never attained, is thus always deferred. However, it is once again a specific sort of deferral: always repositioned, reconsidered, reoriented and thus renewed. One always fails and starts again, but rather than despair, this failure generates new action in an echo of Beckett's "fail again, fail better."

Moreover, in the context of queers and surrealism, however, this ideality is more than an individual psychic formulation; it partakes of the social because it is shaped collectively, in small

13 "Je crois à la résolution future de ces deux états, en apparence si contradictoires, que sont le rêve et la réalité, en une sorte de réalité absolue, de *surréalité*, si l'on peut ainsi dire. C'est à sa conquête que je vais, certain de n'y pas parvenir mais trop insoucieux de ma mort pour ne pas supporter un peu les joies d'une telle possession." (*Manifeste*, 24)

groups, and this adds a particularity to it. Such a dedication to the social dynamics and implications of subjectivity will be central to my discussion here because it is the best possible response to Drew Daniel's questioning of Muñoz's conception of the utopian horizon when he inquires: "are there easy to trace collective experiences and behaviours and affects that treat 'the scene' rather than 'the person' as the essential level of description? Are there queer forms that already formally enact the collectivity and ephemerality that Muñoz stakes his hopes upon?" (328). The challenge remains, as Muñoz wrote in an essay on punk, "to look to queerness as a mode of 'being-with' that defies social conventions and conformism and is innately heretical yet still desirous for the world" (*Gimme Gimme*, 96).

That said, this embrace of an ever deferred paradise opens the interpretive door very wide, and legitimates new ways of reading the movement as practical forms of *movement*. They show us that the protean nature of either (or both) the queer and the surrealist project makes it/them susceptible to approaches beyond the hermeneutic; it is responsive to epistemology and affect, to politics and even to erotics. They suggest that the key to understanding the movement lies not in analysis exclusively, but in synthesis, not in isolating themes, ideas or tropes but in knitting them together and tugging at the connections. That intuition, in fact, lies at the heart of the current project, my attempt to theorize a kind of Queer Surrealism, because queerness, specifically its articulation in the early years of Gay Liberation (and in the work of that moment's heirs) has a similarly sweeping ambition: a desire to transform politics, culture, notions of gender and intimate relationships of love and desire at one fell swoop. Thus my concern here will be to review the current literature with an eye concerned not so much with exegesis alone, but with synthesis and – beyond that – generativity. I want to see not merely where the writing has gone and how it connects, but what those connections might open up, where they might lead. Some of the subtle lines of force joining these accounts are clear even from this brief consideration of their programmes. My argument, however, – by building on the work of Munõz, Tim Dean and others – attempts to articulate even more fundamental connections and commonalities in order to theorize the ways in which both models, by predicating their endpoint as a perpetually displaced and utopian horizon – whether the "surreal" or the "queer" – whose very unattainability is a generative engine, leads them to create *practices of the self* that are simultaneously psychic and social, and that open on new forms of community, and a host of other practices as well.

Such openness is vital because it not only recognizes past work and accomplishments by both surrealism and scholarship, but it acknowledges that – despite any number of critical obituaries – the movement continues to thrive in the present day ("active surrealist groups and individuals circle the globe from London to Buenos Aires, Stockholm to San Francisco, Prague to Portland) and creates space to investigate how such past work might inform future investigations, including my own.

CHAPTER 2
EROS

Thus, both surrealist and queer liberationist practices predicate as their endpoint a perpetually displaced utopian horizon – the "surreal" or the "queer" – whose very unattainability is a generative engine. Some important issues necessarily arise from such a paradox, most prominent among them the manner in which such a frank sidelining of the question of achievability situates the whole value of the horizon in its pursuit. So conceived, a horizon is necessarily, and always, an object of perpetually renewed desire. And from this arises another matter: what, consequently, is the nature of desire, of *eros*, in such a context? The pursuit of an ever-unattainable utopian horizon must at least partly "[manifest] itself as the revolutionary yearning for an entirely different way of loving and another kind of society. Thereby it remains faithful to what is *yet to come*" (Han, 46, emphasis mine).

This "yet to come" cannot be other than the "a-telos" of Munõz's vision in all of its complexity, which requires a broadened understanding of the potential of the erotic, one as complex as the urge to the utopian itself: a conception that understands eros as simultaneously a psychic and a social force – as a power capable of transforming all manner of relationships, including that between self and other, and that with the social and material world. If "[s]ex or the libido characterizes a certain energy, drive, passion, or enthusiasm for the object of one's desire.[...] with directionality, excess, and release of energy" and "[....] takes one outside of oneself" while "[p]ower, by contrast, arises out of concrete relations with others" (Silverman, *Philosophy*, 1) then eros, the rush of energy towards some *other*, structures both individual subjects and the times, spaces, and contexts (social and political) of their intersection. This vision is foundational for any theorization of a Queer Surrealism, which requires a conceptualization of eros as something that is simultaneously: (a) a force in the world; (b) some form of structuring principle for experience; and (c) a matrix of relationality in both the intimate realm and the larger world.

Silverman's characterization of the libido as directional and excessive points to the centrality of the erotic conceived of here as an energy or force. And, insofar as both surrealism and gay liberation have been informed in foundational ways by psychoanalytic ideas, their conceptions of eros reflect to various degrees Freud's insights regarding erotic feelings as "psychical accompaniments of biological processes" (*New Introductory Lectures*, 119) that "[arise] from sources of stimulation within the body [and operate] as a constant force [which] the subject cannot avoid [...] a certain quota of energy which presses in a particular direction" (120). This conception of the libido as being intrinsic to life itself is tightly woven through the thought of both movements examined here; surrealists and gay liberationists alike start from the assumption that the libido is a psychic drive, rooted in the unconscious mind and thus a *material* affective reality with *concrete effects*. They recognize that erotic impulses prompt us to action, underpinning or prompting, for example, the whole range of our choices and decisions, but they further recognize the way in which it also informs our perceptions, which is to say our understanding and experience of reality itself. The necessary correlative of this is that a Queer Surrealist eros (or a surrealist, or a queer, eros, for that matter) implies the subject's relationship to the world is fundamentally an erotic one, making more specific relationships merely an instance of a larger principle.

In this way eros becomes a sort of underlying force, or matrix, for relationality itself. It becomes the substance through which any subject meets the object – of whatever sort – of its attentions/intentions. Han writes, in an insightful reading of Badiou with resonant implications for the notion, of love as a "two scene," "[i]nterrupting the isolated perspective of the One, [and making] the world arise anew from the vantage point of the *Other*, or *Difference*. Love, as an experience and an encounter, is marked by the negativity of upheaval: 'It is clear that under the effect of a loving encounter, if I want to be really faithful to it, I must completely rework my ordinary way of 'living' [*habiter*] my situation" (44-45). Thus eros, as a passionate form of love, not only enables, but requires a transformed relationship to the other, whether an individual, an object in the world, or the world itself.

For the surrealists, eros, the affective complex of love and desire, is a force capable of uniting people and dissolving oppositions. In their work, it is a power that unveils the marvellous and nourishes a capacity to transform the world; desire is "at the core of their utopian vision" (Finkelstein, 77). Surrealist eros also shares something with Lacan's understanding of desire as relational, as a "relation of desire to desire [...] the desire of the other" (*Concepts*, 235) which is to say as dialectical and invested in the mutual recognition of self and other, a situation fraught with productive tensions (I recognize you, you recognize me) that make the experience a "reservoir of energy" (Székely, 116) in which "[t]he crux of surrealist love is a blending, but not a unification of these drives" (115) and where "the struggle of Eros [...] exemplifies this most basic dichotomy i.e. between life and death drives – with the spectrum of other supposed contradictory relations with which the surrealists were endlessly preoccupied (e.g. thought/action, dream/waking, real/imagined, past/future, reason/madness [...]" (115). For surrealists then desire, as a place of encounter and reconciliation, is an experiential model for the utopian horizon of surreality itself; love, particularly passionate love, is a "primary relational model," (Sakolsky, 16) and a force that structures experience and underpins connection in all its forms, and such an understanding is elaborated at length in the movement's works across disciplines and media.

So, as an immanent force or energy and the matrix underlying relationality, eros becomes a structuring principle: not simply a way of coming to people, things and objects but a way of making sense of them, a way of organizing them, interpreting them, tracing their contours and significances as they arise and pass through us. The documents left to us by the writers and artists of both the surrealist movement and gay liberation testify to this in the clearest imaginable way; therefore let us pass on to the consideration of some such texts.

An examination of the archive/canon of surrealist works is sufficient to establish precisely how central desire is to the movement's worldview. The theme is inescapable in surrealist writing; no comparable avant-garde grouping shows such continued interest in both love poetry and pornography. The year 1928 alone saw the Paris group begin a series of remarkably frank round table discussions of sexuality that would continue until 1932, and the appearance of three major erotic works: *Mad Balls* by Benjamin Peret, *Irene's Cunt* by Louis Aragon and Georges Bataille's notorious *Story of the Eye*. A mere two years later, in 1930, Luis Buñuel's then-scandalously erotic surrealist film, *L'Age d'Or*, would first be screened. In addition to eros' ubiquity in the writing, the movement made it the guiding theme of their 1959 International Exhibition which featured 75 artists from 19 countries including Man Ray, Dorothea Tanning, Joseph Cornell, Louise Nevelson and the Quebecer Jean Benoit in his now canonical performance work "The Execution of the Testament of the Marquis de Sade" (Mahon, 154-155). Moreover, the catalogue of the exhibition included this notice to visitors by Breton: "The only art worthy of man and of space, the only one capable of leading him further than the stars... is eroticism." (Cited by Mahon, 143) The conjunction here of being led to a goal with the appearance of stars is telling; it evokes the notion of a "guiding star" and navigation, or the charting of a course through the world. It suggests the extent to which the surrealists see eros as sufficiently important to serve as the basis for the new order and way of life they seek to create. Moreover, the image of the star is central to Breton's war-era work, *Arcanum 17*, in which he endeavours to chart a course for surrealism after the massive destruction wreaked across Europe during the conflict.

MAD LOVE, CRYSTALLINE STRUCTURES AND THE TRANSFORMATIONS OF DESIRE

However ubiquitous desire may be in the surrealist canon, there are a number of texts that turn a particularly keen eye on the matter; Breton's prose work *Mad Love* is surely among them. Though the book comprises an explicit theorization of surrealist desire, its composition as an interwoven collection of narrative fragments, theoretical reflections and reminiscences, make it difficult to classify by genre. Moreover, Breton explores love, sexuality, beauty and passion in the book while taking such feelings in the broadest conceivable sense, further complicating attempts to categorize it. In addition to human relationships, he considers the pull of places and the irrational fascination provoked by certain objects that have the power to "enlarge the universe, causing it to relinquish some of its opacity" (15).[14] This interest in an affective relationship to objects suggests the breadth of Breton's understanding of the matter and is of sufficient importance that it will be considered in some detail later. Here however, the focus will be on the book's analysis of the attachment that develops between people; "this love, *the bearer of the greatest hopes* [...] I am hard-pressed to see what

14   "[...] d'agrandir l'univers, de le faire revenir partiellement sur son opacité," (*L'amour fou*, 21-22).

could stop it from winning out in conditions of life as they might be renewed" (92, emphasis in the original).[15] Statements of this sort, which are characteristic of *Mad Love*, suggest the social/political significance Breton sees in eros, a position well aligned with the surrealist programme overall, since the group had, from its inception, defined itself as "specialists in Revolt" (Breton et al., "Declaration," 240). The political import of love and desire was very much a concern for surrealists in the 1930s; the tract/manifesto accompanying a screening of Luis Buñuel's *L'Age d'Or* in which the group affirmed that "[…] Love demands the sacrifice of every other value: status, family and honour. And the failure of Love within the social framework leads to Revolt" (Breton et al., *L'Age D'Or*, 328)[16], makes the case explicit. Moreover, Breton positions such feeling as being vital in navigating what he calls, in a subtle nod to Baudelaire made more explicit in the translator's rendition , the "forest of symbols" (15)[17], the network of correspondences between the mind and the phenomenal world so important to surrealist conceptions of reality. In doing this the text suggests that love-desire is simultaneously an energy, the "life force […] and its own supposed polarity" as Székely states (113), and a method of using that energy to structure life and relationships, a complexity requiring a close parsing of the text on both the formal and thematic levels.

15 "cet amour, *porteur des plus grandes espérances* […] je vois mal ce qui l'empêcherait de vaincre dans des conditions de vie renouvelées" (*L'amour fou*, 135-136, emphasis in the original.)
16 ".. l'Amour, […] qui demande qu'on lui sacrifie tout : situation, honneur, mais dont l'échec dans l'organisation sociale introduit le sentiment de révolte." (*l'Âge d'or*, 24)
17 "Forêt d'indices" (*L'amour fou*, 22).

Mad Love's intricately facetted and recursive structure makes space for various aspects of erotic feeling to be treated repeatedly and resituated in the larger field of experience with Breton returning notably to their specifically psychic and political import. Of course, imagistic (and analytic) proliferation and reconfiguration marks much of Breton's work and is liberally represented in his poetry, notably in one of his most celebrated poems, "Free Union" with its cataloguing of the various parts or facets of his lover. It would be difficult not to envisage the poet examining the beloved bit by bit, with each facet held up to the light in appreciation and an attempt to locate a certain enchantment, in lines such as "Woman of mine with woodfire hair/With thoughts like flashes of heat lightning/With an hourglass waist/Woman of mine with an otterlike waist between the tiger's teeth" (1-4).[18] However the construction of *Mad Love* takes proliferation past simple imagery and into the realm of form, highlighting the text's interest in larger structures of desire and the manners in which *they are experienced*.

Of his own experience of the power of love-desire Breton writes thus:

I have never ceased to identify the flesh of the being I loved and the snow of the peaks in the rising sun. I have tried only to know the hours of love's triumph, whose necklace I here clasp about your throat. Even the black pearl, the last one, I am sure you will understand

18   "Ma femme à la chevelure de feu de bois/Aux pensées d'éclairs de chaleur/À la taille de sablier/ Ma femme à la taille de loutre entre les dents du tigre" (*L'Union libre*, 1 - 4)

what weakness attaches me to it, what supreme hope of conjuration I have placed on it. I do not deny that love has a difference with life. I say it should vanquish, and in order to do so, should rise to such a poetic consciousness of itself that every hostile thing it meets should melt in the hearth of its own splendor. *(Mad Love,* 114-116)[19]

Breton's insistence in this passage on "love's triumph" specifically through "consciousness of itself" emphasizes the degrees to which, for surrealism, desire is a form of knowledge and a kind of action, specifically a kind of action in which "triumph" is a possible outcome, which is to say a struggle. The emphasis given to the simultaneity of love and life accentuates such an implication while declaring the centrality of eros to Breton's worldview, but it is the closing affirmation of the passage in which "every hostile thing should melt" that confirms to the poet's sense of love as revolutionary force, capable of overcoming opposition at not merely the emotional and personal level, but in the larger, and social, world. So central to the book's theorizing is this broadly political sense of the import of eros that "Breton's philosophy of love [...] is an idea of love staged in the terms of revolutionary politics, a love which does not so much combine the personal with the

19   "Je n'en ai jamais démérité, je n'ai jamais cessé de ne faire qu'un de la chair de l'être que j'aime et de la neige des cimes au soleil levant. De l'amour je n'ai voulu connaître que les heures de triomphe, dont je ferme ici le collier sur vous. Même la perle noire, la dernière, je suis sur que vous comprendrez quelle faiblesse m'y attache, quel suprême espoir de *conjuration* j'ai mis en elle. Je ne nie pas que l'amour ait maille à partir avec la vie. Je dis qu'il doit vaincre et pour cela s'être élevé à une telle conscience poétique de lui-même que tout ce qu'il rencontre nécessairement d'hostile se fonde au foyer de sa propre gloire" (*L'amour fou,* 171-172)

political as ignore any distinction between them," (Bellin, 7). Moreover, the belief is reiterated time and again in the text, another instance of its recursive and crystalline construction, notably in this passage: "I have never ceased to believe that among all the states through which humans can pass, love is the greatest supplier of solutions [...] being at the same time in itself the ideal place for the joining and fusion of these solutions" (*Mad Love*, 42).[20] Here Breton breaks from the conception of desire as necessarily disruptive or antisocial, of affective life as being in need of governance and opposed to reason and moral agency, in favour of the surrealist conception of human mental life as fuelled by tensions that are productive. As Mahon has observed: "[T]he surrealists broke with Freud's insistence on the need to control Eros and instead claimed that it should be deliberately unleashed for subversive, political ends" (15).

Moreover, if eros is understood as a kind of creative and transformational tension operating between people in *Mad Love*, Breton is not ready to grant that its efficacy stops there, suggesting instead a far vaster ontological and phenomenological range for the operations of passionate response. Breton gestures to this expanded conception of eros a full five years before the writing of *Mad Love* in his response to a questionnaire published by the Yugoslav Surrealist Group in 1932 when he characterizes desire as "the medium through which nature generally makes itself known to man, affecting him in relation to what is (and at the same time, to what is

20   Je n'ai jamais cessé de croire que l'amour, entre tous les états par lesquels l'homme peut passer, est le plus grand pourvoyeur en matière de solutions de ce genre, tout en étant lui-même le lieu idéal de jonction, de fusion de ces solutions" (*L'amour fou*, 63-64).

not) and through which it expresses itself spontaneously to him as a fully formed imperative, encompassing all beings, real or potential at the same time" (cited in Mundy, "Letters," 16). Thus, an ongoing investment in, and investigation of, love and desire led the surrealist movement to conceive of desire as a power capable of both provoking and harmonizing social, aesthetic, perceptual and psychic contraries.

> [I]t is there – right in the depths of the human crucible, in this paradoxical region where the fusion of two beings who have really chosen each other renders to all things the lost colours of the times of ancient suns, where however, loneliness rages also, in one of nature's fantasies which, around the Alaskan craters, demands that under the ashes there remains snow [...] (*Mad Love*, 8)[21]

Breton here points to the extent to which desire and love cannot only bind the social (two beings) together, but also hold emotional forces (loneliness and fusion) and the forces of nature in harmonious tension (ashes and snow). This ontological and epistemological conception underpins what Michael Székely has noted: "the surrealist conception of love is marked by a bias towards the broadening of Eros, eroticism, itself. That is, surrealist eroticism is not only convulsive, it is expansive" (114).

21   "C'est là,tout au fond du creuset humain, en cette région paradoxale où la fusion de deux êtres qui se sont réellement choisis restitue à toutes choses les couleurs perdues du temps des anciens soleils, où pourtant aussi la solitude fait rage par une de ces fantaisies de la nature qui, autour des cratères de l'Alaska, veut que la neige demeure sous la cendre [...]" (*L'amour fou*, 12).

The real import of this conception of eros operating as a psychic force animating the world (and the experience of the world) while empowering relationality, however, takes a particularly striking form in one of *Mad Love's* most renowned passages. In Chapter 4 of the book, Breton offers an important case study: an account of what is called "The Night of the Sunflower" which is a nearly perfect account of the operations of *nachträglichkeit*, Freud's notion of "afterwardness" or "deferedness"(Eickhoff, *Modernity*, 1461-1462) in which previously unknown or unrecognized meanings spontaneously become suddenly clear and conscious at some point later in time. On that night Breton meets and falls passionately in love with a woman of whom it seems he has been dreamily aware, without being conscious of it, for eleven years (67). He comes to this realization when the woman's sudden appearance reminds him of an automatic poem he wrote more than a decade earlier, entitled "Sunflower," which – over the course of the chapter – he decodes to reveal a number of lines that seem to forecast, in the manner of a fortune teller, their meeting and romance (54-64). He takes the image of the "traveler walking on tiptoe" as a prefiguration of this new woman and the unusual figuration "summer-fall" as predictive of the summer dusk during which he encounters her. He feels the poem's evocation of despair references the deep sadness he was feeling at the time of the encounter and takes the reference to the "ball of innocents" as identifying the Ossuary of the Innocents neighbouring the *Tour Saint-Jacques* which was the vicinity of their meeting. The poem's evocation of the *Pont au Change* is, he claims, an almost exact forecast of the situation. Line by line, his close reading of the poem details the curious web of coincidence that brings them together; it explores the network of time, place, and affect underlying the encounter and works to establish a continuity between material forces and those of the psyche that is transformational and signifying. In this way, the incident, and the book's account of it, constitute a remarkable affirmation of a specifically surrealist vision of a transformed – or illuminated – experience of life and the world including the experience of the erotic that, in Cohen's words "validates one of the great dreams of surrealist praxis, that repressed desire does not simply manifest itself through the events of the external world but in fact *produces* them" (157). Moreover, it is in the workings of such a connection between psychic and material life that it becomes possible to view the erotic as a social and transformational power.

Extrapolating from this conception of life and mind overlapping, Breton is able to elaborate two of surrealism's central theoretical objects: objective chance and convulsive beauty. Objective chance for Breton was a kind of principle of "agency [...] an acceptance of the fact that we have a responsibility for the world", (Kadri *et al*, 144) and one that:

allowed for the realization of unconscious desires, or perhaps of desires that were not even unconscious but that only come into existence through the operation of chance. This answered the determination of the surrealists not to be mere poets, concerned with the productions of texts, but to act under the imperative drawn from Lautréamont, that 'poetry must lead somewhere' (145).

Objective chance was, in short, a principle meant to explain the mechanisms of odd coincidences and what might otherwise appear to be marvels or supernatural events in materialist terms: an explanation of how inner necessity interacts with external forces or necessities. It "gives evidence of how surrealism considers reality to be layered, in such a way that events occur not so much on the basis of cause and effect but due to an underlying necessity that can be revealed through openness to its structures" (153). Convulsive beauty is tied to this resolution of internal and external necessities as it dialectically links both terms of such an equation to desire, but also to the extent that it embodies surrealism's utopian quest for a state that reconciles all forms of binaries: "By asserting beauty *must* be convulsive Breton hoists the idea out of its dominant understandings and into a set of associations that make it available for correspondence with other key Surrealist concepts (automatism, the image, objective chance, love and most significantly the marvellous – which Breton also explicitly associates with beauty in the *First Manifesto*: "Only the marvellous is beautiful," etc.) Thus it is situated at the heart of Surrealism's proposed resolution of opposing states," (Fijalkowski 182-183) which is to say its utopian horizon.

Significantly, *Mad Love* embodies this conception of eros as an energy and a matrix for relationality in its very form. The book opens with a curious image: a play or performance, featuring a row of black-clad men and a row of women. Initially the two groups are simply mentioned, but the mention

[41]

is quickly elaborated into a more complex description of the groups as seated across from and facing each other: a spatial image of the dialectic, which is to say a particular arrangement of energy; connected, but in a condition of tension fraught with the erotic. The men, Breton suggests, may be versions of himself and the women those he has loved over the course of his life. This possibility foreshadows the book's central themes and the way in which they will be unfolded. Breton returns time and again to single incidents and people, examining them from different angles in order to tease out various significances, echoing the ways in which a new beloved can haunt a lover, giving familiar things new import, and reframing one's personal narrative. However, although Bellin correctly infers that "the text's work will be to conjecture a redemption of the past by remembering it, by recounting, and by interpreting it" (Bellin, 5), the implication that the row of shadowy women are all *facets* of the beloved is significant for reasons beyond any thematic concern with simple memory. The notion – and the image – of *facets*, of crystalline structure, will become one of the book's central motifs, partly determining its sense on levels both conceptual and formal.

In the very first chapter the author affirms "[t]here could be no higher artistic teaching than that of the crystal.The work of art, just like any fragment of human life considered in its deepest meaning, seems to me devoid of value if it does not offer the hardness, the rigidity, the regularity, the luster on every interior and exterior facet, of the crystal." (*Mad Love*, 11).[22] Thus, the highly organized structure of crystals in the natural world, sequentially revealing one face or aspect after another as it is handled, offers an apposite analogy for the strength of eros as an organizing principle for both the social and the book itself.

This concern with crystals, or crystalline form structures the book; each chapter "begin[s] from, and return[s] to, moments in a narrated life which exists primarily as a point of departure, as implicit structure behind them" (Bellin, 2) and which are considered from a variety of different angles. Thus "*Mad Love* will disjoin and pluralize the putative present of its narration [into] moments which are always already from the past, and recount them in an impossible simultaneous co-presence" (5) creating a crystalline, recursive and proliferating construct of feeling and meaning in which desire is both pursued and actualized in every individual instant. Thus, the development of the opening image itself in which first a row of men is conjured, then a row of women, and then the rows are repositioned and redescribed: a facetted structure in which the image itself is multiplied and repositioned. It is desire *as a force that structures experience* that is evoked in the book's opening image, as a way making sense of the complexity and abundance contained in the book.

Breton will reiterate this approach throughout the text; for

22   "Nul plus haute enseignement artistique ne me paraît pouvoir être reçu que du cristal. L'oeuvre d'art, au même titre d'ailleurs que tel fragment de la vie humaine considérée dans sa signification la plus grave, me paraît dénuée de valeur si elle ne présente pas la dureté, la rigidité, la régularité, le lustre sur toutes ses faces extérieures, intérieures, du cristal" (*L'amour fou*, 16-17).

example, in Chapter 3, which deals with the power of objects to attract and enchant, will introduce Giacometti's difficulty in completing a sculpture, then segue to the sculptor's discovery of a mask in a flea market and Breton's own purchase of an odd, wooden spoon, to then return to the way in which the mask solved a formal issue in Giacometti's work. This is an arrangement that not only replicates the tug of desire and interest but also creates a sequence of revelations.

EROTICISM, EYEBALLS AND THE LIMITS OF TRANS-GRESSION

But Breton is not the sole Surrealist to articulate an expansive vision of eros; his rival in the movement (and chief theoretical interlocutor) Georges Bataille espouses a not unrelated conception when he writes of erotic feeling as: " […] the blending and fusion of separate objects. It leads us to eternity, it leads us to death, and through death to continuity" (*Erotism*, 25)[23], a vision of a mutable – but *connected* – universe that echoes Breton's sense of the interpenetrability of things, although in a somewhat less orderly fashion perhaps. Bataille holds to a conception of eros more rooted in transgression, focussed on fetishism and obsession: a surrealist focus that, as Amos Vogel has noted, aims to "destroy all censors and to liberate man's libidinal, anarchist, and 'marvellous' impulses from all restraint" (460). In this, he is more ready to foreground the tense mutual pull of the life and death drives which tends

23   "à la confusion des objets distincts. Elle nous mène à l'éternité, elle nous mène à la mort, et par la mort, à la continuité " (*L'érotisme*, 32).

to operate more subterraneously in Breton's oeuvre, although "the work of both [...] exemplifies the surrealist grappling with the somewhat paradoxical and Heraclitean relationship between these two forces" (Székely, 115).

Such distinctions aside, in his early novel *Story of the Eye* Bataille creates an almost unique erotic work fusing a scatological sense of the body with a complex system of interlocking metaphors that appear, in their own way, crystalline. It dramatizes the pursuit of the outer limits of the possibilities of experience by the narrator, a young man in a turbulent relationship with a girl named Simone and – initially – another, Marcelle, who appears to suffer from some form of emotional trouble or mental illness and who ultimately takes her own life.

From its opening scenes, the book overlays a transgressive presentation of sexuality with a filigree of trope and wordplay in which metaphor and metonymy transmute and trade places, suggesting the endless displacements of the object of desire. In the first chapter, the protagonists share a curiously intense sexual encounter; Simone, dressed in a fetishistic ensemble of black pinafore and stockings sits in a saucer of milk so her genitals soak in the liquid. While doing so she proclaims (in the translation) "[m]ilk is for the pussy, isn't it," (4)[24] establishing the first in a series of metaphorical correspondences/ substitutions that will dominate the book. This series includes interlocking references to the genitals, eggs, the sun and the titular eyeball – correspondences that necessarily recall the

24   The original French uses an analogous, though untranslatable, sexual word play or pun about "sitting" on things. "Les assiettes, c'est fait pour s'asseoir, n'est-ce pas?" (*Histoire de l'œil*, 51).

importance of the "forest of symbols" Breton points to in *Mad Love* (15) and which he sees as essential in the relationship of psyche to the world mediated by desire. As Hoyles notes, the various erotic games that are the substance of *Story of the Eye* all "originate in word-play [...] It is word play of this kind, cumulative and recapitulative, which structures Bataille's text" (62-63). Thus, Bataille's pornographic tale, however different in tone and content from Breton's hybrid text, shares with it a deep investment in the structures tying subjectivity to broader forces, linguistic, symbolic, and social.

Not surprisingly given the book's title, the eye is central to the vibrating web of correspondences Bataille sets up. Over the course of the novel an intricate series of substitutions of the eyeball will operate as a metonym for the shifting metamorphosis of eros in the relationship between the narrator and Simone. Early in the book Simone's erotic fixation on eggs is established:

That was the period when Simone developed a mania for breaking eggs with her ass. She would do a headstand on an armchair in the parlour [...] while I jerked off in order to come in her face. I would put the egg right on the hole in her ass, and she would skillfully amuse herself by shaking it in the deep crack of her buttocks. The moment my jizm shot out and trickled down her eyes, her buttocks would squeeze together and she would come while I smeared my face abundantly in her ass." (10-11)[25]

The egg, symbolic of life, ties this image to the larger conception of eros – a fact given more emphasis as Simone's obsession grows and transforms, bringing the egg back to the surface later in the fiction. In a scene following a debilitating accident the pair fantasizes about the then hospitalized object of their obsession, Marcelle, and the egg fetish takes on greater complexity: "At that time, we imagined Marcelle, with her dress tucked up, but her body covered and her feet shod: we would put her in a bath tub filled with fresh eggs, and she would pee while crushing them" (36).[26] However, the fascination with eggs goes beyond the realm of Simone's fantasies in an imagistic move that adumbrates the next series of transformations of the complex of symbols. Bataille writes, "It was after such dreams that Simone would ask me to bed her down on blankets by the toilet and she would rest her head on the rim of the bowl and fix her *wide eyes* on the *white eggs*"

25 "De cette époque, Simone contracta la manie de casser des œufs avec son cul. Elle se plaçait pour cela la tête sur le siège d'un fauteuil du salon, le dos contre le dossier, les jambes repliées vers moi qui me branlais pour la foutre dans la figure. Je plaçais alors l'œuf juste au-dessus du trou du cul et elle s'amusait habilement en l'agitant dans la fente profonde des fesses. Au moment où le foutre commençait à jaillir et à ruisseler sur ses yeux, les fesses se serraient, cassaient l'œuf et elle jouissait pendant que je me barbouillais la figure dans son cul avec un souillure abondante." (*Ibid*, 54-56).
26 "En même temps, nous imaginions de coucher un jour Marcelle re-troussée, mais chaussée et couverte encore de sa robe, dans un baignoire à demi pleine d'œufs frais au milieu de l'écrasement desquels elle ferait pipi. (*Ibid*, 74).

(37, emphasis in the original).[27] Here the text begins a central metamorphosis, creating a parallel between eyes and eggs rooted in the erotic: "eyes" become "eggs," another instance of the narrative's deployment of the word play Hoyles notes.

Moreover, the transformations of the egg and eye are given ontological significance at a number of points in the novel, achieving cosmic significance in this passage:

> I stretched out in the grass, my skull on a large, flat rock and my eyes staring straight up at the milky way, that strange breach of astral sperm and heavenly urine across the cranial vault formed by the ring of constellations: that open crack at the summit of the sky, apparently made of ammoniacal vapours shining in the immensity (in empty space, where they burst forth absurdly like a rooster's crow in total silence), a broken egg, a broken eye [...] (48)[28]

This vision of the universe as throbbing with erotic power recalls and deepens Breton's sense of the relationship between subjectivity and the world, the way in which the one shapes and

27 "C'est après de tels rêves que Simone me priait de la coucher sur des couvertures auprès du water-closet au-dessus duquel elle penchait son visage en reposant ses bras sure les bord de la cuvette, afin de fixer sur les *œufs* des *yeux* grands ouverts." (Ibid, 74, emphasis in the original)
28 "Je m'allongeai à ce moment dans l'herbe, le crâne sur une grande pierre plate et les yeux ouverte juste sous la voie lactée, étrange trouée de sperme astral et d'urine céleste à travers la voûte crânienne formée par le cercle des constellations: cette fêlure ouverte au sommet du ciel et composée apparement de vapeurs ammoniacales devenues brillantes dans l'immensité – dans l'espace vide oû elles se déchirent absurdement comme un cri de coq en plein silence – un œuf, un œil crevés [...]" (Ibid, 80)

drives the other forward through the mechanisms of longing. On the diegetic level, however, the transformation of egg to eye to cosmos and back foreshadows and creates a metaphorical field of possibility for the novel's climax: the enucleation of the matador Granero, which takes the trope to its transgressive limit.

Bataille sets his climactic scene at a bullfight with all the suggestion of sacrifice that implies; as a ritual undertaking intended to reconcile or connect the base world with the divine, it becomes analogous in Bataille's surrealist thought with desire as a matrix of relationship. In establishing the scene, the author builds a powerful juxtaposition of the sun-drenched arena in which the "extreme unreality of the solar blaze was so closely attached to everything happening" (59)[29] and a close, malodorous "shithouse" where "sordid flies whirled about in a sunbeam" (61)[30] and in which the narrator and Simone, agitated by the thought of the testicles of the first bull killed that she had earlier demanded, have furious sex. The insistence on the sun in these sections is significant, since the sun is a third round object analogically related to the egg and eye in the text and one that plays a crucial narrative role in the events of this scene since "little by little the sun's radiance sucked [the narrator and Simone] into an unreality that fitted our malaise" (63).[31] Later, returning to their seats Simone is given the raw bull testicles served on a plate on which – in an echo of the early

29 "extrême irréalité de l'éclat solaire est tellement liée à tout qui eut lieu" (Ibid, 85).
30 "des chiottes puantes où des mouches sordides tourbillonnaient dans un rayon de soleil" (Ibid, 86).
31 "Le rayonnement solaire nous absorbait peu à peu dans une irréalité bien conforme à notre malaise" (Ibid, 88).

scene involving the dish of milk – she wants to sit. The narrator refuses to allow her to do so in so public a venue and Simone, overcome by the spectacle of the bullfight, subsequently inserts one of the testicles into her vagina at the very moment the bull gores Granero and dislodges his eye. This simultaneity creates a disquieting parallel as one round bodily part is inserted into a body while another is pulled from one, figuring in some ways the central surrealist idea of the interpenetrability of the world and the self. Bataille further highlights the parallel when the next chapter opens on this self-reflexive note:

> Thus two globes of equal size and consistency had suddenly been propelled in opposite directions at once. One, the white ball of the bull, had thrust into the 'pink and dark' cunt that Simone had bared in the crowd; the other, a human eye, had spurted from Granero's head with the same force as a bundle of innards from a belly. This coincidence, tied to death and to a sort of urinary liquefaction of the sky, first brought us back to Marcelle […] (65)[32]

The stressing of the simultaneity of the action foregrounds the metaphorical and psychic connection between the two

---

32 "Ainsi deux globes de consistance et de grandeur analogues avaient été brusquement animés d'un mouvement simultané et contraire; l'un, couille blanche de taureau était entré dans le cul 'rose et noir', dénudé dans la foule, de Simone; l'autre, œil humain, avait jailli hors du visage de Granero avec la même force qu'un paquet d'entrailles jaillit hors du ventre. Cette coincidence étant liée à la mort et à une sorte de liquéfaction urinaire du ciel, nous rapprocha pour la première fois de *Marcelle*" (Ibid, 88-89).

objects while the reference to the liquefaction of the sky raises two other important points. First, it creates a symbolic linkage of both globular objects with the sun whose presence has dominated the descriptions of the scene, and second, it raises the significance of a second symbolic motif whose presence has been nearly as central to the novel as that of eggs/eyes/balls: that of liquidity and gelatinousness.

Story of the Eye is, metaphorically speaking, drowning in liquids; there are frequent and reiterated references to milk, urine, tears and bodily fluids as well as to the containers holding them: the toilet bowl, the saucer. Moreover, these liquids are frequently tied to the sky and the sun (or other globular objects) as they are in the passage cited above. In his study of the novel, Patrick Ffrench reads this symbolic confluence thus, "[l]iquidity, or liquefaction, provides a second chain of associations which is applied to that of roundness. Liquefaction is the movement of contiguity between the objects whose roundness signifies their being limited. Liquefaction transgresses and ruins those limits" (95). Moreover, the linkage established between the tropes is symbolically apposite as a liquid necessarily takes the shape of its container highlighting, even necessitating, the transformation of the recurring globular objects over the course of the novel and highlighting the connections between them, most significantly the final transformation which can arguably be read as closing the symbolic circle.

Following the events at the *corrida* the pair, accompanied by their new companion Sir Edmund, travel to Seville where they sexually assault and kill a priest at a church appropriately founded by "Don Juan," yet another conjunction of death and sacrifice with desire. In the aftermath of the crime, the narrator finds himself facing something he imagines "[he] had been waiting for in the same way that a guillotine waits for a neck to slice. [He] even felt as if [his] eyes were bulging from my head, erectile with horror: in Simone's hairy vagina, [he] saw the wan blue eye of Marcelle, gazing at [him] through tears of urine" (*Story*, 84).[33] Here the simultaneity of eye, the proverbial window of the soul, which "like the sun, [is] a symbol of the Enlightenment" for Hoyles (62), because of its powers of discernment and ability to make distinctions, egg, and testicle achieve a final state uniting high and low, the noblest and the most base, suggesting that all of the narrative's transformations and transgressions were leading to this moment: the shattered limit of experience which must, necessarily take place after the sacrifice of the bull fight.

What underlies these turbulent substitutions and transformations is an insight profoundly related to that which underpins, however different the books may be, Breton's theorizing in *Mad Love:* the sense that eros, while being a feeling of attraction or desire between two people, is more than merely that; it is a structuring principle, a set of connections, a way of making sense of the world, and one that both intertwines everything and renders it all legible. Eros is as much verb as noun, not simply something one has or feels, but something one does; one uses it to navigate the world, to

33"j'attendais depuis toujours de la même façon qu'une guillotine attend u n cou à trancher. Il me semblait même que mes yeux me sortaient de la tête comme s'ils étaient érectiles à force d'horreur; je vis exactement dans le va- gin velu de *Simone,* l'œil bleu pâle de *Marcelle* qui me regardait en pleurant des larmes d'urine." (Ibid, 99).

understand experience, to establish networks of relationship and make choices, and in Bataille's conception, articulated in his elaboration of "erotism," it is an affirmation of life and experience to their very limits.

LIBERATION AND LIBERTINISM

Though the generative role of same-sex desire in the construction of gay identities and queer cultures is evident, the complexity and the potential inherent in such desire as intuited and understood by radical queers is less so. For many liberationist writers and thinkers, desire is, as it is for the surrealists, more than simply a drive: it is a kind of energy and a privileged space, the locus of an encounter: the place where the individual *meets the other* and *knows* him, whether that be a lover or a community. This was asserted from the earliest moments of the movement as is testified to in Carl Wittman's 1969-1970 *A Gay Manifesto*, a document coeval with the Stonewall riots themselves, and in which he writes the following concerning sexuality's expressive and communicative possibilities:

> *What sex is*: It is both creative expression and communication: good when it is either, and better when it is both. [...] I like to think of good sex in terms of playing the violin: with both people on one level seeing the other body as an object capable of creating beauty when they play it well; and on a second level the players communicating through their mutual production and appreciation of beauty. (74)

This insight, which like Breton's understanding links eros with the aesthetic, is echoed and taken further in the work of another gay liberationist, Charles Shively, whose own manifesto makes the case bluntly: "Our desires are not false, nor an expression of hunger, appetite, want: our desires – to suck cock for instance – are creative, they are the road to creating, to the modification of reality" (263). What is made clear in such assertions is a sense that, contrary to most conceptions, sexuality is not simply a private matter, a physical and psychic drive separate from the main substance of life, but a force that operates at personal, psychic, cultural, and social levels. Desire and romantic passion are seen as acts that create and / or transform one's experience of life and one's place in it: which is to say they transform society.

Furthermore, this understanding of desire as a force with the capacity to reinvent social relations is extended beyond the merely intimate realm by gay liberation as it is by surrealism. One of the earliest gay radicals, Harry Hay, who began his work with communist organizations and the Mattachine Society, the 1950s precursor to the radical forms of liberationist politics to emerge in the late 1960s, conceived of homosexual desire itself as operating in ways incompatible with the patriarchal and capitalist social order. He conceived of homosexuality as involving a subject-SUBJECT consciousness with deep radical potential:

We must re-examine every system of thought heretofore developed, every Hetero-male-evolved subject-OBJECT philosophy, science, religion, mythology, political system, language – divesting them every one of their binary subject-object base and re-inserting a subject-SUBJECT relation. Confronted with the loving-sharing consensus of subject-SUBJECT relationships, *all Authoritarianism must vanish.*" (Hay, 260-261, emphasis Hay's).

Hay's claims here are significant; he asserts a sort of shared subjectivity with significant echoes of surrealism's vision of a world imbued with meaning and responsive to desire. Moreover, the power of desire to subvert hierarchical conceptions and constructions of the social is present in much radical liberationist thought; Shively for example, wrote in the previously cited "Indiscriminate Promiscuity as an Act of Revolution": "Release all the armor [...] We must be open at all times for sexual activity; in fact not make it an in-between action, but make every action sexual." (262). Claims of this sort make assertions analogous to Breton's in their vision of a world in which social and psychological barriers collapse and what were once perceived as discrete times and spaces, overflow into one another in non-binaristic ways. Elizabeth Freeman, who has done groundbreaking work on queer temporality, has also underlined the relationship between queer desire and the phenomenology of time: "It is [....] this wide-ranging sense [of] the uses of the erotic that allows queer and temporality to touch one another across what otherwise might seem a vast conceptual gulf" (159).

Underlying the claims of Wittman, Shively, and Hay is a clear conception of the erotic as a force with simultaneously psychic and social significance and, more importantly, effects.

One possible case of this is taken up in Tim Dean's *Unlimited Intimacy: Reflections of the Subculture of Barebacking*. The book explores – in a rigorously nonjudgemental way – the emergence of a subculture of gay men focussed on the practice of a conscious and deliberate pursuit of hyperpromiscuity and unprotected (condom-free) anal sex. Though a single sexual taste might seem insufficient to anchor a fully realized community in some ways, barebackers see condomless penetration as symbolically and affectively complex. They conceive of it as offering them not only greater intimacy, but also as being a kind of performance art with many other functions, like: "embracing risk as a test of masculinity, counterphobically reinterpreting the pathogen as desireable, diminishing fear of HIV / AIDS [and] eliminating anxiety by purposefully arranging seroconversion, and resisting mainstream health norms" among them (51). This characterization of sexual exploration as a kind of "performance art" suggests that the culture of barebacking is a continuation or development of the radical culture of sex created in the first decade of gay liberation by gay men and which Patrick Moore has characterized as "using flesh and spirit and sexual energy as their artistic tools. The sex of the 1970s was creative; it was art [...] The men of the 1970s seemed to be reaching for something that was beyond both physical release and political freedom" (13). Thus there is a historical, creative, and philosophical tradition underlying such practices and testifying to their social and cultural significance.

Dean also identifies another key value at the centre of the subculture: the way in which the practice of barebacking generates profound social bonds: "By organizing viral transmission as a purposeful activity, barebackers infer that a shared bodily substance – whether conceived in terms of blood, DNA, or HIV – represents the basis for not only community, but also, more profoundly, kinship" (*Unlimited*, 84). In other words, barebackers see themselves as connected to one another in creative ways that, although they replicate the patterns of the consanguineous family structure of the mainstream heterosexual world, do so in a peculiar, and transgressive, register. It is this attempt to move beyond established social arrangements that mark this subculture as at least unconsciously utopian, as a challenge to the normative boundaries of the everyday social world; it is another attempt to reach the far horizon of queerness. However, this "performative" attempt is enmeshed with still another challenge to normativity whose extension is laden with phenomenological and epistemological import.

Arguing that the radical promiscuity of barebackers necessarily takes an oppositional position to the mainstream gay movement's focus on marriage and inclusion in heteronormative familial and other social structures – in ways one could see as analogous to the radical postures of early gay liberation two generations back – Dean examines the philosophical ramifications of the subculture's bodily practices. He contends that in their organized embrace of promiscuity and impersonal sex and the sort of aimless cruising involved in that pursuit, barebackers are articulating a new ethics, rooted in pleasure certainly, but also in openness to alterity or "strangeness" which becomes a sort of openness to the world itself (210-211). This embrace of cruising as a way of life too might be characterized as a utopian vision of enlarged possibilities deeply rooted in both gay men's sexual history post-Stonewall, and in a vision of its possible future transformations; one that resonates with surrealism's pursuit of a broader sense of the world.

JOHN RECHY, PROMISCUITY AND THE POLITICAL

A related iteration of queer sexuality as politically relevant, and oppositional in nature, can be found in the work of gay author John Rechy who has explored the psychic textures of desire, and of promiscuity in particular, across the full range of his substantial *corpus*. Rechy is best known for his 1963 pre-Stonewall novel *City of Night* in which he explores the experience of a young hustler in the then scarcely visible demimonde of gay sex in cities across the U.S. In that book, Rechy's exploration is limned in dense, stream of consciousness first-person prose like this:

Later I would think of America as one vast City of Night stretching gaudily from Times Square to Hollywood Boulevard – jukebox-winking, rock-n-roll moaning: America at night fusing its darkcities into the unmistakable shape of loneliness.

Remembering Pershing Square and the apathetic palmtrees. Central Park and the frantic shadows. Movie Theatres in the angry morning-hours. And wounded Chicago streets... Horrormovie courtyards in the French Quarter – tawdry Mardi Gras floats with clowns tossing out glass beads, passing dumbly like life itself… Remembering rock-n-roll sexmusic blasting from jukeboxes leering obscenely, blinking manycolored along the streets of America strung like a cheap necklace from 42nd Street to Market Street, San Francisco …

One-night sex and cigarette smoke and rooms squashed in by loneliness…

And I would remember lives lived out darkly in that vast City of Night, from all-night movies to Beverly Hills mansions (9).

Such passages, laden with sex, longing, and sadness clearly find their immediate progenitors in the work of the Beat writers, but the headlong rush and collapsing of words one into the other (darkcities, or sexmusic) as well as the condensation and displacement of time and space unmistakably suggest the impact of the turbulence and restlessness of surrealist automatism on those Beat authors; Kerouac's "spontaneous prose" and Burroughs' "cut ups" being, after all, related exercises in the liberation of language. However thick the sense of longing in *City of Night* and other novels, Rechy makes the case for the social, even revolutionary, impact of desire most overtly in his *Sexual Outlaw*, where he writes this: "The promiscuous homosexual is a sexual revolutionary. Each moment of his outlaw existence he confronts repressive laws, repressive 'morality.' Parks, alleys, subway tunnels, garages, streets – these are the battlefields" (*Outlaw*, 28). Rechy's implication is clear: acts of love and desire are not simply able to transform intimate relationships, when deployed properly they have the power to transform the nexus of relationship itself: the social order.

The protagonists of both *City of Night* and *The Sexual Outlaw* are muscular, conventionally masculine men who make their living at least partly by hustling tricks and who bear striking, and acknowledged, similarities to the author himself, and both novels contain a great many explicit sexual descriptions. Despite such similarities the books are structured in different ways; however lyrical, *City of Night* is a more conventional novel composed of a series of set pieces and tableaux while *The Sexual Outlaw* is presented as a "prose documentary" despite the equally insistent lyricism of its pages.

This documentary structure was the subject of Manuel Betancourt's article "Cruising and Screening John: John Rechy's *The Sexual Outlaw*, Documentary Form and Gay Politics." In the article Betancourt investigates Rechy's abundant use of textual versions of the conventions of documentary film such as explicit scene setting via time and place indicators such as "1:04 PM. Santa Monica. The Beach" and labelling some passages as "Voice Over" and others as "Mixed Media." One effect of this, he suggests, is that "Rechy's desiring gazes become constitutive of the documentary image" (32), implying once again a larger – and objective – social role for desire. Such a conviction is further bolstered by the novel's broad range of sensual detail regarding landscape, affect, and the sensations of individual sex acts which provide the reader with both a sense of the "facts" of an encounter and their subjective content effectively transferring, as it were, the narrator's political anger to the reader himself:

obliging him to take such anger, and the positions to which they give rise, as "real" as "facts." Obliging her, in fact, to share "[t]he process of making all public spaces already into sexual outlaw arenas [that] [encapsulate] Rechy's political convictions that the private and the public are disingenuous categories imposed to maintain a heavily circumscribed sexual hierarchy" (44) and "blurring the line between the reality of Jim's sexual hunting and our own process of reading the text" (45). Once again, love-desire and sexuality are construed of as something one does to transform meaning across registers of experience and as part of relationship building.

Of course, the subjective account/documentary divide runs two ways and the blurring of the line serves a number of literary and political motives. Kevin Arnold has noted a tendency in this work that is not unrelated to the argument regarding the textual strategies of *Mad Love* above, writing that, "in giving articulation to this fantasy and at the same time telling us that it is 'documentary' or true, I think Rechy is playing into a reader's desire for this fantasy as a structure of knowledge and desire" (*Male and Male*, 118). Here, as in Breton's account of his obsessive desire (and the tireless cruising of Rechy's protagonist is nothing if not obsessive) the import of desire as a structuring agent for experience becomes salient once again. For Rechy too, the prompting of eros is a legitimate way of plotting a course through the world, of making sense of it, a fact given added emphasis by the use of a protagonist who is also a prostitute: someone for whom the telling of stories and the creation of an image of desire is, in the most literal of manners, a way of making one's way in the world. However, and this is central, in all such cases eros is more than personal it is "defined by subjective positionality and in excess of it" (122) linking it again, processually and ontologically to Muñoz's libidinally beckoning and receding horizon.

FIGURING DESIRE

Rechy's borrowing of structural elements from film is a strategy shared with gay male writers like Jack Fritscher who names the large sections of his historical novel about radical queer sexuality in San Francisco in the '70s *Some Dance to Remember* "Reels," suggesting the shorter chapters comprising them be read as "Scenes," and who structures his erotic short story "Corporal in Charge of Taking Care of Captain O'Malley" entirely as a film script. The simultaneous use of filmic techniques and language points to an interest, among some gay writers at least, in the formal properties of narrative art in general and the ways in which they can structure both the experiences captured in them and the experience of reading itself. But it also opens up the question of how the erotic and its potentialities are handled in surrealist and queer cinema. Two films whose very titles declare their investment in the erotic will prove elucidating in this regard: Luis Buñuel's *That Obscure Object of Desire* and David Kittredge's *Pornography: a Thriller*.

In her early book *Figures of Desire: A Theory and Analysis of Surrealist Film* Linda Williams offers an intriguing reading of *That Obscure Object of Desire* in which she suggests that in this late career (1977) film, Buñuel returns to his earliest, surrealist concerns marked by an "obsessively narrow focus, metaphoric structure, and parody of psychoanalytic discourse – all of which have an affinity with *Un Chien Andalou*," (154). The film, an adaptation of Pierre Loüy's novel *La Femme et le Pantin*, follows the tumultuous pursuit of a young woman Concha (sometimes played by Carole Bouquet and sometimes by Angela Molina) by the sexually obsessed Mathieu (Fernando Rey). The narrative is framed by Mathieu's account of this relationship to his fellow travellers onboard a train and the various incidents he describes are depicted in flashback sequences. The account is precipitated by Mathieu's pouring water over a young woman on the platform: a young woman he describes as "the worst of all women" and deserving of what she received because of the way she tormented him, leading him on while never yielding to his desires. Mathieu's narrative is prompted by one passenger, a little person with a Freud-style beard who is a professor of psychology and who asks for an explanation for such a strange action.

This triggering moment is a clear choice by Buñuel to situate the action in a context reminiscent of the psychoanalytical encounter and thus point to that discourse as a possible tool for reading the film as, in William's characterization, "an amusing parody of the dirty-story aspect of the analysand's cathartic purge" (188). Here Buñuel harkens back to the fundamental role of psychoanalytic theory as a source for surrealist interest in the unconscious, free association and the operation(s) of desire. The account, however, being public insofar as it is offered to a group of fellow travellers sharing the same cabin, renders the situation more complex than a simple therapeutic intervention by adding a social level to it; here, eros (an account of desire) once again acts as a social force, bringing people together in ways removed from the merely sexual – uniting them in a community of interest. Nor is this the only trace of the social in the film and its layered narratives; the action is set against a background of revolutionary violence in which a number of bombs go off. Though the specific details of the revolt (its motivations, actors, and goals) remain obscure, the explosions are reiterated at a number of points in the film providing a counterpoint to the explosiveness of the intimate relationship at its heart.

Concha, the object of desire at the centre of the film, is also the principal figure standing for the obscurity in the title. Throughout the film she remains distant, untouchable even strange: a metonym for the "distance or gap between subject and object [needed] for desire to come into play" (193). Concha appears and disappears with an apparent effortlessness. At first she is Mathieu's maid, but she vanishes when he begins to pressure her too strongly only to turn up in Switzerland later or on the train platform in Seville at the film's opening. Moreover, she seems related in unexplained ways to the revolutionary violence in the film; the bombings and robberies often seem to coincide with Mathieu's sexual advances. The strangeness and uncertainty around Concha's character, however, is given its greatest force by the fact that two different actresses play her, something that goes apparently unrecognized by her pursuer. This is the clearest possible indication of both the obscurity of the object and the reasons for it; what is most important here is the desire itself, the force of it and its effects, and not necessarily any specific object which – as the title states – is always obscure anyway. Happily, Buñuel undercuts the possible misogyny of this by emphasizing not simply the force of Mathieu's desire, but his ridiculousness; time and again he will be portrayed as yearning, but foolish, blinded and driven ever onward by his need in pursuit of an unobtainable vision. Such a contrast creates, not only the ambiguity that haunts the film's perpetual shifts, but also its power as a narrative, its constant rubbing out and repositioning of the forms of the social

The very train that is the film's setting is an operative metaphor for the power of desire, hurtling forward and vaguely phallic in shape, it even – in a particularly broad moment – goes through the requisite tunnel closing the Freudian circle. Moreover, its relentless forward propulsion makes it a convincing trope of the pursuit of a goal, however shifting. Troubling any simple reading of this, however, is the fact that Concha herself rides the train too, unbeknownst to Mathieu and his companions, suggesting once again that the object of desire is only, and can only be, desire itself as a force, as an experience, and can only be self-justifying.

David Kittredge's 2014 film *Pornography: A Thriller* takes a number of similar themes and tropes in order to update — and queer — them. A complex, intricately constructed and open-ended feature, Kittredge's movie is a series of three inter-locking narratives about a vanished porn star that blends elements of the ghost story, slasher film, and mystery narrative. In the first section porn star Mark Anton (Jared Grey), who is attempting to retire from the business, is offered the opportunity to do a private video for a special client in exchange for $40,000.00. Unable to decline, Anton goes to the location and speaks to a camera and intercom until he balks, refusing to cooperate with a demand, and is assaulted by a mysterious masked figure never to be heard from again. In the second section, which takes place 14 years later, Michael (Matthew Montgomery) and his partner move into a loft that they discover once had camcorders installed all over it. Michael, who is writing a book about gay porn, discovers a tape hidden in a wall that seems to depict a young man being tortured and killed by the aforementioned masked figure. The tape breaks while being played, and Michael seeks the assistance of a friend who runs a video shop to repair it. At this point dream sequences and supernatural elements begin to intrude into the film and the sense of the real becomes fuzzy. At a moment of great tension the third section begins. Porn star Matt Stevens (Pete Scherer) is violently shaken by a nightmare and awakens to write, in one sitting and at white heat, a screenplay about a character named Mark Anton that replicates the film's first sequence. As he attempts to get it made he discovers Anton was a real person who disappeared and increasingly strange, even inexplicable things begin to happen around him.

The film's anti natural, arguably surrealist-influenced, elements were widely noted when it was released. Several gay publications, including Britain's *Boyz* and *Just Out* made direct comparisons of the movie to the work of David Lynch, who – though not a surrealist *per se* – borrows heavily from techniques and approaches first deployed by surrealists. *Pornography's* use of these techniques explores, as does *Obscure Object*, the power of desire to shape our experience and relationship to the world. As in Buñuel's film, actors play multiple roles or the same character might be portrayed by more than one player, blurring questions of time, space and identity. In a classic surrealist gesture the line between reality, dream, and representation is troubled or eliminated by the reiteration of scenes and the passage of people and events from one diegetic level to another, as in moments when events that were simply typed up suddenly happen in the "real time" of the film. The three narratives are given complex formal treatment in the film through the extensive use of dream sequences, interpolated "video footage," the reiteration of identical lines of dialogue (often laden with connotative import such as "I don't know if the face in the mirror is mine," "You want me to be real?" or "Is this what you want to see") by different characters, unresolved plot elements, repeated symbols (crossword puzzles, a ring bearing a strange sigil) and a lack of clarity regarding whether the masked figure is real or not. Such techniques, which, if they are occasionally heavy-handed are very well deployed, work to heighten the film's thematic explorations of its central themes: the relationship between reality and the imagination, the scopophilic impulse and the power of obsession most prominently. Furthermore, like *Obscure Object*, the importance of the narrative act – the account – is foregrounded; rather than a verbal account set in a parodic psychoanalytic context; however, *Pornography* sets its events in the world of writing and movie-making suggesting once again that desire, when given form, shapes both the individual and the world he inhabits with consequences that are simultaneously psychic and material.

Of course, the complex and expansive understanding of the power of love and desire was not exclusive to the surrealists and the gay liberationists; the roots of the notion are in Freud and there have been vastly influential works exploring these ideas since; one need only note the impact of Marcuse's *Eros and Civilization* on the post-war counterculture for example, which certainly fed into the work of gay liberationists. However, few other currents of thought have approached the question of eros quite so deliberately, so programmatically, as these two tendencies. What Han has written of surrealism, I would contend of the liberationists as well; for them eros is "the medium of a poetic revolution in language and existence. It is exalted as the energetic source of renewal, which also feeds political action. Through its universal power it combines the artistic, the existential and the political" (46). It is in this expansiveness that the potential of a Queer Surrealism lies: specifically, in providing one specific, concrete context for the understanding that eros is more than something we feel inside, that it is a way in which we relate to others and the world, and hence it is something we *do:* an insight that might well explain the repeated analogies drawn by these groups between erotic activity and, for example, playing the violin and other forms of creative work. Desire is an action and a structure for action, and done with enough care, enough consciousness, enough craft it can become a practice. After all, to borrow from Hammers "[...] queer sex is radical, not for what it annihilates, but rather for what it spawns. Queer sex is radical because it is productive of queer relations, which is the crucial engine for queer politics and resistance. That is, queer 'ways of relating' reconfigure, and thus challenge, normative hetero-relational arrangements, thus generating in turn alternative community formations"

(845), and such relations in turn generate our images of the world, which is to say *our world* and our ways of inhabiting and responding to it which brings us to questions of affect and *aesthesis*.

CHAPTER 3
AESTHESIS

Surrealism has opposed reductive epistemological binaries from its beginnings; foundational statements like the following, from the *Second Manifesto*, stake out the position most clearly: "Everything tends to make us believe that there exists a certain point of the mind at which life and death, the real and the imagined, past and future, the communicable and the incommunicable, high and low, cease to be perceived as contradictions" (123).[34] Though the statement is widely known, and commented on, comparatively few critics have lent the closing phrase the attention it deserves given its importance. At first glance, it might appear that the movement is opposed to the rational, and to reasonable approaches to life and the world, championing instead unreason. However, such a reading is an oversimplification and one that continues to underpin some critical assessments. The *Manifesto*'s assertion is not an either/or proposition. The surrealist project is far more complex than any simple inversion of conventional binarisms as many participants would reiterate at different points in the

34   "Tout porte à croire qu'il existe un certain point de l'esprit d'où la vie et la mort, le réel et l'imaginaire, le passé et le futur, le communicable et l'incommunicable, le haut et le bas cessent d'être perçus contradictoire-ment." (*Second manifeste*, 72-73)

movement's history. Breton himself is clear on this; in another declaration (also cited above), for example, he writes, "I believe in the future resolution of these two states, dream and reality, which are seemingly so contradictory, into a kind of absolute reality, a surreality, if one may so speak" (*Manifesto*, 14).[35] Benjamin Peret, another major surrealist, is as direct when he denounces the "artificial opposition between poetic thought and logical thought, between rational and irrational thought" (Peret. Cited in Matthews, 85) as is Bataille in his *Inner Experience* when he writes, echoing Breton's statement, of the "possibility of uniting *at a precise point* two types of knowledge which up to now had either been unknown to one another or only roughly brought together" (xxxiii, emphasis in original).[36] The vision of a state in which binaries are resolved clearly undercuts any idea of oppositionality, including – most importantly for our work here – that between reason and unreason or thought and feeling which is to say between *noesis* and *aesthesis*, because as Conley notes in "Sleeping Gods," "[p]art of the surrealists' purpose [...] was to destabilize the unified Cartesian notion of identity as a salient feature of the human being, based on thought" (8). Therefore, this chapter examines *aesthesis*, which is to say feeling and sensitivity, the ability to perceive or experience sensation, and its association with intellection (*noesis*) in the cultural production of surrealism and the gay liberation movement and its heirs. I will attempt to formulate a model of

35   "Je crois à la résolution future de ces deux états, en apparence si contradictoires, que sont le rêve et la réalité, en une sorte de réalité absolue, de *surréalité*, si l'on peut ainsi dire." (*Manifeste*, 24)
36   "*La possibilité d'unir* en un point précis *deux sortes de connaissance jusqu'ici ou étrangères l'une à l'autre ou confondues grossièrement...*" (*L'expérience intérieure*, 11)

aesthesis that does not exclude forms of intellection while also attempting to determine the ways in which it might structure a variety of relationships: primary operations of consciousness; the relationship to the material world and material objects in the world, and the relationship to, or sense of, the self.

For a Queer Surrealism the complex relationship between language and consciousness will necessarily be dynamic and fluid, operating generatively on levels beyond questions of denotation and symbolic reasoning with a profound investment in the material reality of language and its power to *embody* thought: to give it particular and deployable form. Thus its work will embrace a conception of language as a process, as movement and flow, and focus its attention on such linguistic attributes as metaphor, analogy, and the whole range of figurative possibilities as simultaneously affective and representational strategies that make meaning from the encounter of perception and feeling, which are understood as continuous, feeding into one another through forms: verbal, material and human.

In such a context representation itself becomes charged with potential and energy. It blurs semiotic and semantic divisions and categories such as icon and index in favour of a wider field of sense and troubles the line between consciousness and the world while fostering a sense of the *continuous*, of the underlying continuity of things. Persons and objects, the self and the social, however discrete, are *felt* or *perceived* to be connected and thus, epistemologically, *are* connected, at least at the level of experience, an experience that, as has been discussed, is erotic in nature. Thus Conley's observation of the surrealist interest in "destabilizing the unified Cartesian" subject is pertinent and could, in fact, be taken further. In foregrounding such a dynamic conception of consciousness a Queer Surrealism works towards a sense of self that is not simply "destabilized" but fluid, plural and generative. Moreover, leveraging aesthesis in this way, valuing affect and perception as modalities, upturns teleology, creating an open-ended knowledge that values response and exchange rather than analysis alone; in this way it empowers the perpetual repositioning of the utopian horizon and its attendant possibilities, and it is these possibilities that animate the very representations that surrealists and gay liberationists have put to work in their practices and politics, beginning with their inaugural manifestoes themselves.

In light of this, one notes, *The Second Manifesto* does not assert that differences do not exist between life and death or past and future, only that the mind has the capacity to stop seeing them as oppositional: the power to resolve them on some level or another, and that is a phenomenological or epistemological assertion, not an ontological one. It is a claim that has to do with perception, affect and relationship, and thus, it becomes necessary to examine the movement's model of consciousness and perception and the ways in which they are understood to operate.

Surrealism's investment in the operations of consciousness begins with a desire to investigate what might be called the interior voice; this was made apparent in the first *Manifesto* itself in which Breton and his cosignatories affirmed flatly that surrealism was "[p]sychic automatism in its pure state by which one proposes to express – verbally, by means of the written word, or in any other manner – the actual functioning of thought. Dictated by thought, in the absence of any control exercised by reason, exempt from any aesthetic or moral concern" (26).[37] This statement goes beyond staking out an intellectual position for surrealism; it proposes a methodology. In this definition "automatism," or the attempt to follow the actual functioning of the mind, is made programmatic. Thus, insofar as the technique is posited in a definition of the movement, Breton lays out both a theory and a practice for surrealism in the *Manifesto*, and he defines that practice as not simply a tool, but as being integral to the very fabric of surrealism. The surrender to the flow of language here, given that the definition specifies immediately that the automatic action is done "in the absence of any control exercised by reason" (26), is an experience of linguistic *sensation*, of aesthesis rather than intellect. Karen Conley picks up on the importance of sensation in automatism and uses the analogy of swimming to characterize the practice and its operations in the body as "an experience of suspended receptivity, on the one hand, and as a ghostly rushing flow of movement, on the other" ("Ghostly Automatic Body," 300). In Conley's reading too, therefore, automatism is both an action and a sensation, an experience making the practice far more than a compositional method.

The automatic techniques the group would explore in pursuit of "surreality" were various and included automatic

37 "Automatisme psychique pur par lequel on se propose d'exprimer, soit verbalement, soit par écrit, soit de toute autre manière, le fonctionnement réel de la pensée. Dictée de la pensée, en l'absence de tout contrôle exercé par la raison, en dehors de toute préoccupation esthétique ou morale." (*Manifeste*, 36).

writing, of course, but also mediumistic trance, the construction of irrational objects, dream transcription, fumage, frottage and decalcomania in visual media, and the playing of games such as the "cadavre exquis" among other things . Though various forms of automatism are given pride of place in declarations by Breton and other prominent surrealist theoreticians, it is most often discussed in terms of automatic writing. Despite the clear centrality of textual *production*, however, one finds discussions of the resultant texts and their formal, political or aesthetic characteristics more rarely in the literature. Therefore, a brief discussion of some such texts may prove a useful starting point for considering their various effects.

SENSATION AND THE AUTOMATIC

Two early works, *Soluble Fish* by Breton and *The Magnetic Fields* by Breton and Soupault, are important examples of automatically generated texts. Though different in significant ways – one is authored by an individual, the other is a collaborative piece, and one shows greater traces of continuity and even narrative than the other – there are striking similarities between the two works. An examination of these shared qualities will show them to be recurring markers of the form.

Soluble Fish offers a series of linked vignettes exploring an emotionally and metaphorically charged landscape. It is composed of a series of imagistic tableaux connected by a density of language and the recurrence of images of fantastical flora and fauna, and of women who are given a charged treatment evoking both longing and a sense of "lost" romantic relationships. As Thompson notes, the trope of women's bodies in *Soluble Fish* "seem[s] to corporeally and abjectively power the twists and turns of the automatic textual flow" (10). These images of the feminine not only create part of the ambiance of the writing but act as anchor points that attract or guide the attention, against which other images, other sentences are weighted or interpreted and which pull the reader along in a kind of tumult of the imagination, suggesting an underlying continuity between the practice of automatic writing and its products. Viewed in this light, the text becomes not so much the record of an experience, but an embodied form of it. These women, arguably images of desire and other sorts of romantic affect for the avowedly heterosexual male authors, also provide a vestigial narrative through-line for the text that, though not continuous, does provide a veneer of what might be called "structure." This passage provides a sense of the ambiance pervading the text:

> Looking back I no longer see clearly, it is as if a waterfall stood between the theater of my life and me, who am not the principal actor in it. [...] I have dreamed of loving her the way one loves in reality. But I have not been able to rid myself completely of half a green lemon, her scull-like hair, the inadvertence of traps for catching animals alive. She is sleeping now, facing the boundlessness of my loves, in front of this mirror that earthly breaths cloud. It is when she is asleep that she really belongs to me; I enter her dream like a thief and I truly lose her as one loses a crown. I am stripped, surely of golden roots,

but I hold the strings of the storm and I keep the wax seals of crime." (*Soluble Fish*, 54)[38]

Passages of this sort, and passages of even greater imagistic density and emotional charge, are the main substance of *Soluble Fish*. Here we see the curious juxtaposition of prose sentence and paragraph with poetic image and metaphorical impulse: there are inadvertent traps and storms bound by strings, golden roots, as well as portentous half-lemons whose significance to a very partial narrative is unclear, and yet seem laden with meaning. We also note the presence of aforementioned mysterious women in the selection who provide a recurring motif in the text, and we see the permeability of the divide separating dream from waking life. Hence, it is pertinent to note the ways in which the passage clearly seems to occupy a place somewhere between a list or catalogue poem and prose sketch. It is also an early example of what would ultimately prove to be vital themes in surrealist writing: the overlap of the natural and psychic worlds, love and desire, and the mutable or transformational potential of reality.

The Magnetic Fields, composed in 1919, is the earliest example of "surrealist" automatic writing. However since it

38 "À distance je ne vois plus clair, c'est comme si une cascade s'interposait entre le théâtre de ma vie et moi qui n'en suis pas le principal acteur. [...] L'aimer, j'y ai songé comme on aime. Mais la moitié d'un citron vert, ses cheveux de rame, l'étourderie des pièges à prendre les bêtes vivantes, je n'ai pu m'en défaire complètement. À présent elle dort, face à l'infini de mes amours, devant cette glace que les souffles terrestres ternissent. C'est quand elle dort qu'elle m'appartient vraiment, j'entre dans son rêve comme un voleur et je la perds vraiment comme on perd une couronne. Je suis dépossédé des racines de l'or, assurément, mais je tiens les fils de la tempête et je garde les cachets de cire du crime," (*Poisson*, 32-33)

precedes the *Manifesto* by several years its characterization as "surrealist writing" is prefigurative in some regards. That said, it prefigures the subsequent importance of automatism for surrealism in compelling ways. We can see its formal and affective links to *Soluble Fish* in this example:

> The moment for meteors has not yet come. The simple rain tumbles down onto the motionless rivers. The malicious sound of the tides proceeds to the labyrinth of moistures. Having been contacted by shooting stars, the anxious eyes of women have closed for several years, They will no longer see anything but the tapestries of the June sky and the high seas; but there are magnificent sounds of vertical catastrophes and historical events." (*The Magnetic Fields*, 40)[39]

In this section too we see the keen attention to the natural world and its metaphoric potential: moisture takes on the structure of a "labyrinth," the sky becomes a "tapestry," "historical events" have sounds. We also note the recurrence of images of women in this text, and in a textual role that parallels the one they play in *Soluble Fish*, providing gravitational centres around which the automatic flow of writing pours. They respond to shooting stars and turn from the June sky and sea, guiding the images

39 "L'heure des météores n'est pas encore venue. La pluie simple s'abat sur les fleuves immobiles. Le bruit malicieux des marées va au labyrinthe d'humidités. Au contact des étoiles filantes, les yeux anxieux des femmes se sont fermés pour plusieurs années. Elles ne verront plus que les tapisseries du ciel de juin et des hautes mers; mais il y a les bruits magnifiques des catastrophes verticales et des événements historiques." (*Champs magnétiques*, 43)

that precede them and those that follow alike. The images of women are centres, or rails along which the flow of metaphor and, significantly, desire itself circulate.

These curious juxtapositions recall the most basic techniques of metaphor: substitution and combination, the power of one thing to become or be another on some distant level of thought or consciousness. This partly explains the prominence of figuration in much surrealist writing with its focus on the capturing of mental activity. However, the importance of metaphor goes far beyond this for Surrealism. Anna Balakian sees great import in the "philosophical significance attributed by the surrealists to the creation of the metaphor. For them it is not a mere form of speech [....] the measure not merely of literary satisfaction but of a victory over ordinary existence" (137). In automatic writing the metaphor becomes a way changing perception and destabilizing fixed conceptions of the world and its operations, a way of "transcend[ing] reason's impression of opposition and inconsistency" (Mathews, 274) or "neutraliz[ing] dichotomies." (Adamowicz. 80.) Unsurprisingly for a group that has characterized itself as "specialists in Revolt" (Breton *et al*, *Declaration*, 240)[40], metaphor is a kind of weapon for surrealism, a way of taking "that supreme step which is the poetic step par excellence: excluding (relatively) the external object as such and considering nature only in its relationship with the inner world of consciousness" (Breton, *Situation*, 260), hence it is a kind of perception or awareness generated through feeling; it is *aesthesis*. And, if Breton is touching here on the disjuncture of poetry and prose he is doing so in conceptual

40   "des spécialistes de la Révolte," (*Declaration*, 219)

terms, not in terms of any purely formal problematics. This is consistent with surrealism's declared strategies since the practice of automatic writing would "[eject] its practitioners from the realm of mundane experience" (Thompson, np) and become a technique for achieving the resolution of dream and reality hoped for in the *Manifesto*. However, it would also produce texts that utterly eliminate the question of poetic form because they are meant to replicate the preconscious source from which they arise, prior to rational form.

Some critics have noted this concern with subjectivity is not always, or necessarily, limited to individual subjectivity. Chénieux-Gendron makes an effective case for reading the highly idiosyncratic text *The Immaculate Conception* as a new breakthrough in surrealist automatism in her essay "Toward a New Definition of Automatism: *L'immaculée Conception*." Despite the work's being written by two different authors and separated into distinct titled sections, including some that are simulations of clinically "disturbed" mental states and another that is constituted of aphorisms, both of which could suggest conscious deliberation, she argues that internal evidence and archival material both confirm that the composition of the text was automatic and that *The Immaculate Conception* marks an enlargement of surrealist ideas of automatism beyond the original notion of taking a kind of dictation from the unconscious by including procedures rooted in their devotion to the idea of "play." Based on her analysis of the original manuscript pages, she suggests the text was constructed by rapid writing on the part of the two participants (Breton and Éluard) and around a series of predetermined prompts constituted by the "titles" and that each writer would immediately respond to the text laid down by the other automatically. Further, both Breton and Éluard were acquainted with psychiatric nosology from their service during World War 1, which would have provided them with the knowledge necessary to "automatically" simulate the various symptoms found in that section of the work. In this way *The Immaculate Conception* marks, for Chénieux-Gendron, an intersubjective automatism resulting from a sort of literary and psychological game; "automatism, in its ultimate phase, thus presents itself as an activity of leisure different from what it was for *Les Champs magnétiques*. And still the playful attitude must be distinguished from hoax [...] [it] implies a poetical engagement of the mind in its entirety." (88).

However, the transgressions of automatism go beyond the idea of the single autonomous author or the prose/verse distinction. Given that automatic writing is intended to be a simple transcription of a continuous verbal flow alive with desire and conceived of as always already present in the unconscious mind, it straddles or interrogates other categorical divisions such as that between fiction and nonfiction or creative writing and documentation. If an automatic text is simply a record of something already existent, the rush of the unconscious monologue, it should of necessity be a document, not a creative artefact and yet it seems both; it is fact not fiction, but it is neither. In some ways the "automatic text becomes a place of recognition and reconciliation" of these conflicting possibilities. (Sherringham, 56); it allows surrealism, as Breton states in "The Surrealist Situation of the Object" (1935), to "[succeed] in *dialectically* reconciling the two terms – perception and representation – that are so violently contradictory for the adult man, and [to] throw a bridge over the abyss that separated them" (278).[41] Thus, the question of the categorical status of such texts, in contradistinction to their content or form, necessarily opens up on a larger matter than that of poetic form, that of genre and the nature of representation itself.

Philosopher and logician Charles Sanders Peirce articulates an organizational model for the various types of signs based on the ways in which they work, the relationship of the particular sign to what is represented. He proposes three basic sorts of signs: icons, which represent based on resemblance to a thing; indices, based on some actual connection of a physical nature; and symbols that operate by some agreed upon convention (10). Thus, if, as has been suggested, an automatic text is not simply the record of an experience, but an embodied form of that experience – the act of writing automatically itself – such a text is an index, physically connected to the writing body and mind. Such a claim could be made for many surrealist techniques: dream recording, for example, or trance generated creation or the playing and results of surrealist games. This is, of course, in keeping with many principles of surrealist epistemology which views reality and dream, and other states of consciousness, as communicating vessels that overlap and spill into one another and reveal themselves through the coincidence of inner necessity and external forces or necessities.

GAY MYTHOLOGIES

41   "d'avoir réussi à concilier *dialectiquement* ces deux termes violemment contradictoires pour l'homme adulte: perception, représentation; d'avoir jeté un pont sur l'abime qui les séparait," (*Situation*, 167-168).

In light of the specificity of such models, some consideration of queer appropriations of automatic techniques is necessary in order to theorize a Queer Surrealism. Although the original Paris group of the Surrealist movement included a number of queer people – René Crevel and Claude Cahun[42] come immediately to mind, as does the more closeted bisexual Louis Aragon – the most out affiliate of modernist era surrealism is surely the American Charles Henri Ford. His 1933 novel *The Young and Evil* (written with Parker Tyler) is a ground-breaking work in English deploying a variety of surrealist techniques including the stream-of-consciousness (or automatist) narration discussed above to depict a very early state in the emergence of an organized gay community. This makes the novel an almost unique document of the significant overlap between queer and surrealist concerns in the early twentieth century. Moreover, See suggests that this appropriation of a method borrowed from "surrealism provide[s] Ford and Tyler[43] the techniques to elude [...] subservience [to reality]" (1093). The reference to escaping reality, however oblique, points to surrealism's "great work," which is the pursuit of surreality itself. Clearly, this refusal of ordinary reality operates on the literary level See deals with, but it also obtains, for surrealists, on the epistemological and affective levels as well. This situates it in the domain of *aesthesis*, particularly since, as Breton states in his remarks on the resolution of binaries, that we are dealing with oppositions in "perception," the mechanism through

42 Cahun in particular has been the subject of much fascinating work in gender studies in recent years, but that focus lies outside of the scope of this project.
43 Parker Tyler, the coauthor of the novel.

which things enter awareness, not intellection. This is a refusal, See acknowledges, that is shared by queers who must regularly confront heteronormative ideas that are frequently binaristic, and thus analytical rather than synthetic, regarding gender, marital status, and sexual identity, among other things.

Also of note in Ford's novel is the play of a clearly camp sensibility which is seen from the book's earliest pages in lines like this: "Well said the wolf to Little Red Riding Hood no sooner was Karel seated in the Round Table than the impossible happened. There before him stood a fairy prince and one of those mythological creatures known as Lesbians. Won't you join our table? they said in sweet chorus" (11). Camp, insofar as it "emphasizes style as a means of self-projection, a conveyor of meaning, and an expression of emotional tone" (Babuscio, cited in Howard, 10) lies squarely within the domain of affect and the operations of consciousness at once. Alexander Howard's approach to *The Young and Evil* ties Ford's use of camp to his poetic theorization of "Imaginationism," "an expressive and stylized poetics of 'personality' and 'self-created laws'" that "are not invented in advance but seem to be created as the poem forms itself" (10). The productive yoking together of stylization and the emergence of "self-created laws" in the process of writing powerfully suggests that Ford's approach constitutes an early queer extension of automatist practice given that any "spontaneously emerging" law would of necessity have been generated automatically.

Though Ford and Tyler's novel offers an early example of the influence of a queer aesthesis based in surrealist automatism it is important to note that such practice has remained an ongoing, if underground, current since. Notable in this more recent genealogy is the work of Ronnie Burk. Burk, a Chicano-American poet, was active in both the Chicano and gay liberation movements over the span of his highly peripatetic life while also developing an astounding body of work blending Mexican themes and imagery and Buddhist philosophy with surrealism. Burk's first exposure to surrealism came through a meeting with Charles Henri Ford himself, who assisted in some of his early publications, but it was American poet Philip Lamantia – himself brought into the movement by André Breton who hailed him as "a voice that rises once in a hundred years" (Caples et al., xxvii) – who was in all likelihood determinant. So central was this encounter to Burk that he would later describe Lamantia as "the biggest influence on his returning to write, desiring to write, and shedding old forms" (Hernández-Ávila).

This influence is given a queer spin in the corpus of poetry Burk created prior to his early death in 2003. Here, for example is "To Wed Fire:"

To wed fire to air: the mercurial sperm must be tossed into the vessel with a pinch of arsenic. A pile of gold dust to tip The Scales of Libra. You've now passed from nigredo to the point of dismemberment. Droplets of black rain on the back of a swan push down skeletons of rotting milkweed. Microwaved. Ravens pick at your remains. A scroll of sheet music to tone the spheres. In the last chapter lions devour each other in Her Majesty's very own audio-hallucinatory fugue. Aleph, that pillar of cloud hovering over The Walls of The Cast-Iron City, told the story of two fat cupids in a glass jar (43).

In this poem, the longing for the unattainable utopian horizon of queerness and surrealism is given form in a series of tense dialectical pairings such as "mercurial sperm" and "arsenic," "black rain" and a "swan," "skeletons" and "milkweed" whose juxtaposition (and, presumably, resolution) within the instructional or recipe narrative implied in the poem ultimately leads to an "aleph," the symbolically loaded first letter of the Hebrew alphabet and hence an image of new beginnings. The aleph, in turn, is described as a "pillar of cloud hovering over the Walls of the Cast-Iron City," an allusion to the Exodus of the Jewish people to the promised land whose utopian valence needs no unpacking. Significantly enough, we are also told at the poem's closing that the aleph told the tale of "two fat cupids in a glass jar" (43). This image with its evocation of a conventional allegory of love and plenitude (fatness) sealed off, and embedded simply in a narrative, further points to the unattainability of the fullness of desire and its function as an account that leads the hearer onward.

A similar sense of desire as a form of practice or pursuit also animates "Your Hair:"

Filigree of sensation
sludge of pain
dirty river of contagion
floating corpses of the Ganga
sewers of sex
My heart sleeps there

covered with lunation cycles
oblivious,
slightly disturbed,
a little paranoid,
a frightened animal held together
with leopard skins & scarabs
My heart sleeps in a velvet current
aching, restless, wanting
only you (60)

Lamantia's influence is visible in the poem's chain
of associative leaps drawn from both natural world and
mythological archive is evident in the reference to scarabs, at
once insects and a prominent symbol in the Egyptian mythos
(one source of Lamantia's imagery) as well as in the evocation
of the Ganges. Such associations, however, are deployed
affectively, in the service of a longing the poem directly situates
in relation to the reader herself and that is depicted as part of
"current" or a flow of sensation, again hinting at an open end
point.

Nearly as significant in Burk's emergence as a poet as the
encounter with Lamantia, were his studies with Beat Generation
luminaries at the Naropa Institute. The Beat poets also constitute,
in fact, one of the important streams transmitting a surrealist-
influenced poetics to the post-war United States. A debt to
surrealist practice is detectable in the three main figures of the
Beat generation: Jack Kerouac, Allen Ginsberg and William S.
Burroughs despite the oppositional position each has taken in
relation to the movement at various times.

Kerouac has described his "spontaneous prose" this way: "[t]ime being of the essence in the purity of speech, sketching language is undisturbed flow from the mind of personal secret idea-words, blowing (as per jazz musician) on subject of image." (*Essentials*, 1). Formulated in this way, his "undisturbed flow from the mind" is clearly analogous, indeed all but indistinguishable from Breton's proposing "to express – verbally, by means of the written word, or in any other manner – the actual functioning of thought" (*Manifesto*, 26) because each understanding stresses the writing down of thought as it arises, and does so for similar reasons: in order to capture the movement of language across an active consciousness. Kerouac's colleague, and fellow Beat paragon, Ginsberg's poetry is marked by a visionary picture of the world rooted in William Blake, Jewish mysticism, and the expansive eros of Whitman and is written in a language strewn with hallucinatory images such as "the machinery of night" and "incomparable blind streets of shuddering cloud and lightning" that clearly echo the juxtapositions characteristic of Breton's championing of "two things whose conjunction would not be permitted by common sense." (*Ascendant Sign*, 104).[44] They are so reminiscent in fact that, as Brian Jackson has noted the poet "viewed himself as one of the true inheritors of Modernism [....] regarding his work as a continuation of the French avant-garde, especially the Surrealism of Antonin Artaud" (298). Burroughs' innovation of the "cut-ups" is a more idiosyncratic development of surrealist techniques: not of automatic writing *per se* in this case, but of

44 "telle chose et telle autre, que le sens commun retiendrait de confront-er," (*Signe ascendant*, 133).

the quintessential surrealist game of "cadavre exquis." Like the game, which required a number of players, each of whom responds to a fragment of text or visual image by adding some words or pencil lines without having seen it in order to ensure the final result (a drawing or sentence) would emerge free of any control of a rational mind, the "cut up" too pursues a random result, but by actually cutting up a text and rearranging it. The goal of such practices is, naturally, the production of previously unapprehended or unrecognized meanings; in "both cutting up texts and [...] writing or drawing the Corpse, the surprise for the practitioner, and the fascination, arises from anticipating the apparently chance production of significance" (Harris, *Cutting Up*, 93). Moreover, Burroughs was introduced to the cut-up by his friend and collaborator Brion Gysin who had briefly been a member of the Paris surrealist group until he was expelled from it in December of 1935, thus establishing another possible specific historical link for the transmission of automatist practice from the original group to the Beats.

Automatic writing, with its focus on the operation of language and consciousness itself, however, was not the surrealists' sole aesthetic practice, nor the only one taken up by queer writers and artists from Stonewall to the present day. Some variations of aesthesis, in fact, took other forms of connection to the material – and social – world as their target. Such broadness is implicit in the practice of automatism itself given how, as has been noted, automatic writing tends to take particular forms and act as both an artefact and a trace of the passage of consciousness.

INDEXICAL OBJECTS

For surrealists, a privileged encounter between consciousness and the world of forms takes place across a broad range of situations and things. This led practitioners, from the late twenties and early thirties on, to take an active interest in the "object" as a phenomenon: found objects, interpreted found objects, and surrealist objects properly so called, which were created in response to a variety of irrational promptings and for a wide range of symbolic functions. Breton himself conceived of the relationship to the object as central to surrealist epistemology; he asserts in "Crisis of the Object" (1936) that it "[entails] nothing less than the objectification of the very act of dreaming, its transformation into reality" (277)[45] which again points to its role in the pursuit of the perpetually deferred horizon of surreality. In this way, objects become the meeting ground of interior and exterior life, privileged loci of relationship, zones of the encounter of forces. As Conley has it, "by having been turned away form their original functions, [surrealist objects] repress their manifest lives and thus generate *champs de force* or force fields through this process of transformation that results from the juxtaposition of the object's current and former realities. In this way, what was formerly manifest becomes latent once it is taken out of its original context […] and this new latency produces energy." ("Sleeping Gods", 10).

This recognition of the potential significance of a variety of objects led the surrealists to surround themselves with things in which they saw such force fields; many of them became serious collectors, most notably André Breton himself. Breton's

45 "n'était rien moins que l'objectivation de l'activité de rêve, son pas-sage dans le réalité" (*Crise de l'objet*, 277)

collection has particular historical and cultural significance, marking as it does an important point in Modernism's concern with African, Oceanic and other traditional cultures, however mediated by colonialism. This aside, our primary interest here is the extent to which collecting such things "can be viewed as a revolutionary and poetic practice within everyday life" (Rudosky, iii), and the extent to which it impacted Breton's writing and the development of surrealism more broadly. Containing thousands of "manmade and natural objects, books, manuscripts and other miscellaneous curiosities and ephemera" (iii) as well as paintings and other works of modern and tribal art, the collection was carefully assembled, considered and arranged in Breton's home (Figure 1) suggesting the central importance it had for the poet and the extent to which he saw it as constitutive of his personal environment on the material and affective levels. Indirectly addressing such connections in his meditation on crystalline forms in *Mad Love*, he wrote, "[t]he house where I live, my life, what I write: I dream that all that might appear from far off like these cubes of rock salt look close up" (11).[46] Breton here suggests that his life, his writing and his home, which was dominated by his collections, should be viewed as continuous, as elements of a larger structure in which the various components complement and reflect one another in order to achieve their fullest expressivity. Nor should the fact that Breton's apartment was his studio, the place in which he made his work be neglected, nor that the objects that surrounded him entered into his compositional practice and

46 "La maison que j'habite, ma vie, ce que j'écris; je rêve que cela apparaisse de loin comme apparaissent de près ces cubes de sel gemme," (*L'amour fou*, 17)

were viewed as "things that connoted use, or function, rather than mere aesthetics" (Mileaf, 252). Indeed, "Breton spoke more than once of his need to be surrounded by his objects and his work, the contemplation of which 'uplifted' him and which he saw as a window opening onto some other thing. He also described the need, when writing, to move about, to touch this or that object to reassure himself of its reality and to make contact with it" (Comina, 82). What emerges from such statements is the surrealist notion of a relationship with the world in which some sort of vital consciousness is shared, or distributed to elements of the material world, in which "[a]ny piece of flotsam and jetsam within our grasp should be considered a precipitate of our desire" (Breton, "Exhibition of Objects," 283).[47] Thus Breton's collection becomes a sort of universe, an aesthetic statement and an element of his poetics at once: a curious status, positioning it very differently from the typical institutional or personal collection whose functions are generally archival and/or investment driven. Moreover, this atypical function of surrealist objects/collections, the way in which they are allocated value, whether poetic or political, is increasingly an object of research and study. Conley has argued that "Breton's thinking became more refined once he began processing his thought by reflecting upon specific objects in his collection" (*Sleeping Gods*, 7) and, elsewhere, that where he "was most free in his own automatic expression may well have been with his collection" ("Surrealism and Outsider Art," 141) making the connection of object and practice truly explicit.

47   Tout épave à portée de nos mains doit être considérée comme un précipité de notre désir," (*Exposition surréaliste d'objets*, 283).

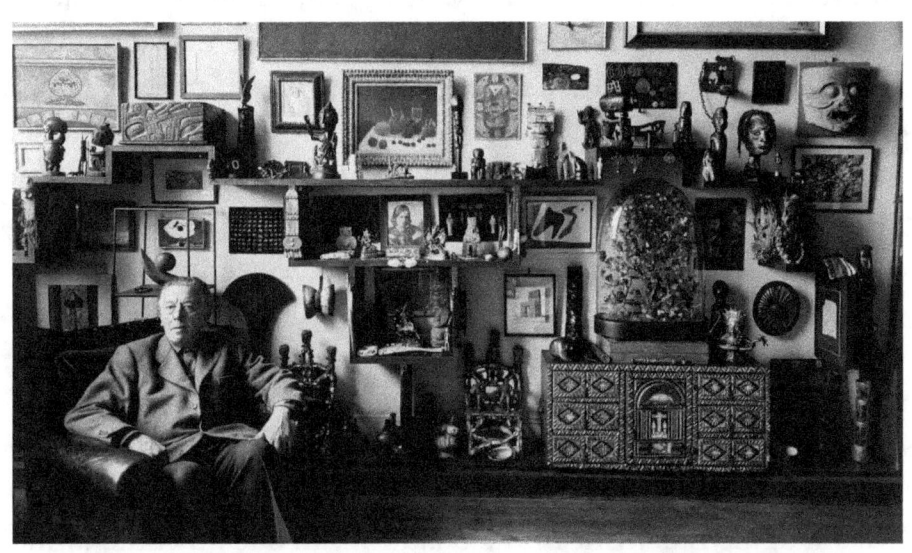
Figure 1. *André Breton with his Collection*, photo by Sabine Weiss, 1955.

The matter of the collection and the "collecting impulse" is another structuring point of contact between surrealism and queer culture, particularly in light of the commonplace trope of the gay "aesthete" or man of taste. This notion, however true or false, of gay men as having a particular interest or competence in the arts emerges in the Victorian period with the career, and fall, of Oscar Wilde and the aesthetic and decadent movements in arts and letters, particularly as expressed in his character Dorian Gray who is driven to ruin by the deliberate cultivation of sensual and aesthetic pleasures. Wilde's promulgation of art for art's sake in a body of work that displayed its subversiveness at least as openly as its concern with beauty led to a deep association of aestheticism with the "cultivation of the senses to the realm of the abnormal and perverse (according to the prevailing moral standards)" (Altick, 297). Moreover, though the idea emerges here, it probably reaches its greatest expansion during the high modernist era in which the perception of gay men's power in the cultural sphere took on conspiratorial shades and a "Homintern" (Sherry, 2007) was imagined at work in the shadows. In such a context, the matter of the relationship to objects and collections of objects becomes a specific case of the general principle, though often an especially salient or contentious one as is testified to by the furor surrounding the sale of Wilde's collections after the bankruptcy precipitated by his trial (Ellmann, 459), or the flurry of interest to emerge after Warhol's death in the artist's compulsive collecting, and the recent sceptical attention given to Samuel Wagstaff's prominence as a collector and his role in the development of Robert Mapplethorpe's career (Gefter,

2014). Questions of general applicability aside, however, there have been a number of important collections amassed by gay men, and one with particular relevance for consideration of the affective politics of collecting is that of Samuel Steward.

Steward's busy life, so carefully documented in Justin Sping's *Secret Historian,* included careers as an academic, author, and tattoo artist as well as collaboration with Dr. Alfred Kinsey on his germinal sex research, and literary friendships (linking him to Parisian modernity and the milieu of the surrealists) with Alice B. Toklas and Gertrude Stein, the latter of whom was an early supporter of his writing: a body of work that includes literary fiction, essays, belles lettres, and pornography.[48] In addition to his professional activities, Steward was an amateur artist (and a professional one if one weighs his tattoo work in the balance) and a dedicated collector.

Steward's collection, an impressive attempt to document or record an entire life in some ways, includes: celebrity autographs; what he referred to a "latriniana," (Spring, 86) or the documentation of dirty jokes and graffiti from men's rooms; homoerotic "fetish objects; objets d'art, curios, books, photographs, and prints" (102) and sex-related disciplinary devices (130). So comprehensive was the collection that Kinsey had Steward's flat photodocumented for the Institute for Sex Research. Along with these objects and documents Steward also compiled his now legendary "Stud File," a meticulously organized, annotated and cross-referenced card catalogue in

48   Tom Waugh notes Steward's connection to the trans-atlantic Modernist avant-garde in his *Hard to Imagine* (106). (He also reflects on Charles Henri Ford in the same context in this work, marking him as an important early commentator on the queer/avant grade tradition.)

which he carefully documented his sex life "in its entirety from 1924 through 1974" (xiii) and which he bolstered by supporting material such as clippings of his partners' pubic hair. These collections, whose thoroughness and single-minded focus on gay sex arguably makes them a unique archive of twentieth century sexual behaviour, especially when one acknowledges the peculiarly generative slipperiness of the notion of the archive in recent critical writing, which has "expanded to cover unofficial, idiosyncratic, and personal collections of material [... and ...] suspend the standard distinction between archive and collection" (Dean, "Steward's Pornography" 31 - 32). Moreover, as Dean notes, these personal collections take on special significance due to their dependence on an indexical function, because the index, he argues, is "the sign of intimacy" (29).

The index is based not simply on likeness, but on "physical connection" (37); it is in some way part of that which is represented; a footprint in relation to a person's body, a weathervane to the direction of the wind, for example. And Steward's collections are filled with indexical signs and items. His collection of pubic hair is clearly so, but his collection of polaroid images of his lovers can also be construed as indexical; they are connected to the men by chemical and other physical processes which transforms the body into image, and by the fact of posing at a specific time and place making them the index of an encounter, and highlighting the way and extent to which indexicality is tied to affect. Nor is his pornographic writing necessarily excluded from such an understanding since it frequently refers directly to the indexical, as in the case of the "dickprint" in the chapter of *Roman Conquests* titled "Passport" discussed by Dean (38 - 39). However, Steward's material has other, more affective and social implications, since almost all of it references his sex life and thus "constitute[s] a unique form of evidence about relation and connection" (42) and works to "[multiply] and [intensify] non-utilitarian pleasures among an ever-shifting community of male partners […] not only to 'memorialize' sexual encounters, as he often put it, but also to provide new ones" (35). The encounters entered his collection, which then fed his fiction, which in turn brought on more encounters in a way that is undeniably analogous to the role of the thousands of objects in Breton's collections: stumbled upon in flea markets, galleries and *brocantes* then entering his work and ultimately the world to generate more *trouvailles*.

Thus, the collection as "index," as tied to feeling, community, memory, and creative action, though discernible in most forms of collecting, becomes peculiarly central here through its implication in broader forms of practice. Steward both commemorated and activated his sex life and community of lovers in this practice and Breton arguably did something similar on a different register. It is necessary to remember in connection with this the insistence with which the surrealists saw their "tribal" and found objects as functional, as tied to the numinous world of surreality, or in the case of African, indigenous American and Oceanic artefacts as tied to the magical world in more traditional understandings. In this way, these objects too had an indexical status, representing a thing because of their proximity or connection to it, to the "other world" in this case: and this enabled their possessors to sense

[97]

or perceive these worlds – they enabled aesthesis. They were stand-ins for their own larger contexts; embodiments of great, encompassing desires. It is this notion of the embodiment of desire that brings us to a practice of aesthesis in which the connection between the object and its representation moves past indexicality and becomes indissociable: self-fashioning.

AFFECT, ASKESIS AND THE AESTHETIC

If a conception of desire as simultaneously a force and a praxis of relationality underlies both queer and surrealist approaches to aesthesis, then body and self must necessarily fall within its purview; the case of Pierre Molinier is exemplary in this regard. One of the prominent postwar adherents to surrealism, Molinier, a painter, photographer, and photo/body artist, was welcomed into the movement by Breton himself who would later organize one of the few gallery shows the artist received during his lifetime. Though first recognized as a painter, Molinier's work in photography and photomontage has drawn most critical attention since his suicide in 1976 and has been widely examined by scholars of gender and sexuality due to its often provocative subject matter. The striking nature of the imagery, its erotic content and curiously ethereal mood, is particularly congruent with the artist's own statements regarding it; Molinier held that "[t]he work of art is the materialization of that which is most intensely felt by each individual" (Cited by Baerwaldt, 11). The insistence on feeling or sensation ties his self-representational project to questions of aesthesis or coming to grips with the world through sensory data rather than simply intellection. The content of the images, moreover, heightens this by an obsessive concern with certain sorts of materials and their contact with the body.

The presence of sensual information in the images is striking; Molinier's visual universe is one in which silky stockings shimmer and cling to an endless parades of legs, in which cross-dressed figures pavane on spike heels and caress themselves and other similarly clad figures, in which they wear masks and veils against the skin, and in which the anus is exposed and repeatedly penetrated even as it presides over the image space. In these images sensual pleasure reigns supreme, and all too often it is Molinier in conventionally feminine clothing experiencing it. He may be alone or accompanied by similarly-dressed others, either human lovers or artificial beings, but he is both the subject and the object of the pictures. His figure, idealized into a kind of transcendent, or infernal, androgynousness by clothing, makeup, and masks is the constant subject of the photos and the underlying spirit of his baroque, supernatural paintings with their suggestions of a universe whose central characteristic is itself change or transformation. Moreover, critics have linked the instability of Molinier's pictorial world – and its implicit philosophical questions – to surrealism's pursuit of a world beyond the ordinary: "Molinier's actions were clearly guided by a savagely subjective eye that intended to bypass the restrictions imposed on the body by a moralizing sensible bourgeois society [without] ' any control by reason,[…] aesthetics or morals'" (Baerwaldt, 14 - 15). In this light the photomontages are, like Breton's and Steward's collections a kind of index: an index of Molinier's pleasure, certainly, since they not only document it but were used in provoking new encounters and pleasures, but of the project of surrealization itself, the attempt to move towards a new relationship with the world, one beyond binaries.

Their pornographic content aside, many of Molinier's photographs bear a more or less conventional relationship to portraiture insofar as they depict a sitter in an ordinary room and/or chair. However, the sitter is a man wearing stockings and garters as well as a mask depicting a heavily made up face, and – oftentimes – involved in sexual acts. When Molinier moves to the construction of photomontages however, the fetishistic content spirals into an entirely different register. In *La rose noire* (*The Black Rose*), (ca 1960) (Figure 2) in which a central figure – masked and veiled – reclines holding their legs in the air, while one sees a scenic ornamental screen in the background behind him (another possible evocation of the unattainable horizon propelling both surrealism and Munōz's conception of queerness, and which certainly underlies Molinier's fetishistic and idealized androgyne). Between the figure's spread legs the eponymous flower protrudes from the anus. More startling than this, however, an anatomically impossible second pair of stocking-clad legs are right behind the first set. The masked face (presumably Molinier) is central, floating between the legs and immediately above the anus, visually linking what one might conceive as the highest point of the body with the most base. A superficially obscene, or pornographic picture, the image in fact conceals the body's erogenous zones, the genitals and anal opening, in favour of highlighting fetishistic and symbolic material. Though this is, on one level, congruent with Freudian understandings of the fetish as a part of the body or some inanimate thing that is substituted for the "normal" sexual object and given a "psychologically essential overvaluation" (Freud, *Reader*, 249-250), the image also operates on levels far removed from those of ordinary individual psychology. By camouflaging and transforming the very things that are central to the image's evocation of desire, the face and the anus, Molinier underlines the mutability of that desire; the anus is a rose, a flower whose symbolic valences are particularly broad, suggesting spiritual beauty and sensual pleasure alike while the wearing of a mask points to both the mutability of identity and the riot of crime and carnival at once. What is depicted is, in many regards, not simply Molinier, but his profound investment in notions of transvestism as *transformation*, in the epistemological possibilities of disguising, or more properly of reshaping the self. The pictures are "[...] [a]n obsessive documentation of the artist's body *anticipated* in stages of transformation." (Baerwaldt, 13). Molinier, "[b]y using the aesthetic construct of fetishism to bridge the [...] unresolvable contradictions between illusionistic representations, unfulfillable desires, and reality" (Gorsen, 41), endeavours to both represent his utopian horizon and draw closer to it. Thus, the work sidesteps many of the psychoanalytic critiques of so-called "perversion" which is often thought to "indicate an incapacity to socialize desire, something that cannot be emphatically stated of Molinier, for in his life and work, while never suppressing his autoeroticism, he spilled out over others, even if only by the (imaginary) device of mirror play" (Aliaga 33). These photomontages, in other words, become sites of knowledge, of an understanding

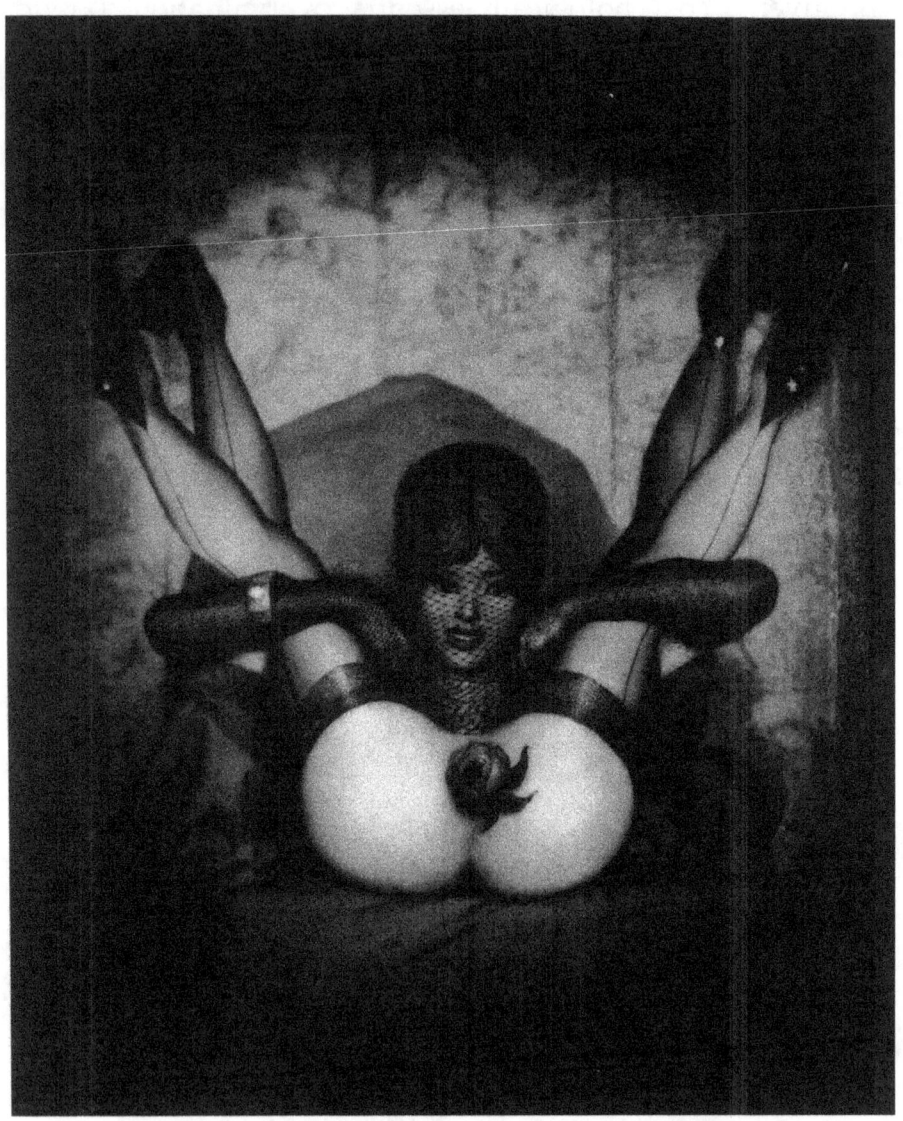

Figure 2. *La rose noire (The Black Rose)*, Pierre Molinier, 1960.

of the world and one's place in it, and the possibilities of the transformation and proliferation of such places.

The 1968 work *Elevation* takes proliferation, extension and transformation yet further. Where *The Black Rose* features a mysterious second pair of legs, *Elevation* represents no less than eight pairs of legs clad in Molinier's beloved sheer stockings and garters. The accumulation of limbs is arranged into something reminiscent of a human pyramid in which a group of four legs forms the base supporting a larger assemblage at the centre of which, once again, is the masked and veiled face. The whole fleshly structure is surrounded by a luminous aura lighter than the dark background in the print. Given the title *Elevation*, the viewer is immediately faced with the question of what is being elevated, particularly since, in this image, what is at the top of the structure is identical to what is at the base. One is reminded of the hermetic and alchemical dictum "that which is above is like that which is below" with its appeal to the continuity of forms and being, particularly given that the teetering structure is composed almost entirely of similar pairs of legs. The only other form in the composition is, once again, the doll-face mask which rests at the centre, more shadowed than the luminous buttocks contrasting so brightly with the black fabric of the stockings. There is a sense, in the tonal contrasts and the possibility of the head being overpowered by the proliferating legs that the conventional hierarchy of mind and body has been overturned and the limbs and organs are what reach out to and take in the universe around the body. Though the head, which is masked and thus – in a sense – negated, is at the centre of the massed forms one must read it in the context

[103]

of the image as part of the assemblage, not its highest point. In this way noiesis, intellection, is dethroned and made part of a larger apparatus in which aesthesis, the awareness of bodily and affective sensation, holds the greater place. That said, the body and the head remain continuous, of one visual substance, regardless of any relative prominence.

This is significant because *Elevation* is an image of both ascent and balance, the legs and buttocks are piled one atop the other in an order (and postures) that appear to defy gravity; *Elevation* constitutes a sharp articulation of the idealizing or aspirational implications behind Molinier's obsessively reprised figure: his vision of an underlying ontological unity that is felt since "for Molinier the physical realm was undifferentiated from an idealized spiritual realm" (Baerwaldt, 9). So great is the sense of bodies joining with, or emanating from, each other that Breton's early statement on the work, suggesting that the fetishistic images and objects (the silk stockings, the sheer veils) can themselves be tokens or vehicles for continuity, takes on its fullest resonance. In these images "[a] silken ladder has at last been thrown from the world of dreams to the other world, which proves conclusively that this other world could only be that of carnal temptation" (*Molinier*, 246).[49]

A related intuition animates the paintings, in which the painterly treatment sometimes tests the line between the figurative and more abstract forms of representation. In *Culminate* (1962), we see this sense of the continuity of existence and the way it responds to the promptings of attention and

49 "Un échelle de soie a pu enfin être jetée du monde des songes a l'autre, dont se trouve ainsi démontré qu'elle ne pouvait être que celle de la tentation charnelle" (*Pierre Molinier*, 246).

desire in a curiously "all over" composition of legs and mouths, hands and lips and eyes, all writhing together in an almost formless ecstasy but doing so before a single recognizable and complete head that presides, watching, over the picture very near the upper right corner; its hovering presence suggests a sort of voyeuristic pleasure in what it perceives, a pleasure that can rightly be called aesthetic since what is at stake is the visual, sensory detail of the amorphous orgy. The head, which reappears in a number of the artist's paintings and is recognizable for the repeated treatment of the makeup, suggests the doll mask Molinier so often wears in his work, adding to the impression that here too it is he in the image. The writhing, and interpenetrating, mass' indistinguishability is further highlighted by the tonal continuity of the image, dominated by tones of peach, pink, orange, and red with framing tones of grey/blue. Given the painting's title, a paradoxical sense of teleology comes to bear on the reading; this, the title insists, is the culmination of some vital process. One has arrived, here at a desired end, in which some subject (the face) realizes itself in the extension of its desire across existence, in situating itself as part of a desiring universe even as it extends ever onward. This is fundamentally beyond simply the extinction of the personality in the erotic; it is rather a realization of it as part of a network of desire, an understanding of the self as fundamentally relational and hence aesthetic and, in light of the sense of process, an ending that opens only on more change.

A similar sense of the self as an aesthetic construction of relationality is equally present in the work of a number of gay artists; most notable in some respects is the case of Peter Berlin who, like Molinier, generally worked with eroticized images of himself.

Much of Berlin's work in film and photography was created within a decade or so of the Stonewall uprising, which is to say very early in the emergence of a public and politicized gay world. These years saw the rapid development of queer political, cultural, and social/sexual organizations and institutions along with a concomitant appearance of openly gay works across disciplines from literature and cinema to visual art, music, and other forms of performance. Although gay writers and filmmakers published and exhibited work that was consumed by gay audiences prior to Stonewall the representations of gay experience were generally heavily coded in the manner of, for example, Tennessee Williams or physique magazines. In the years following the uprising, an explosion of gay imagery appeared that was openly declarative and frequently erotic. Gay audiences of the time were eager for such representations of their lives, experience and bodily practices and consumed such productions in vast quantities; the archive of erotic gay print and visual culture is vast, diverse and tremendously significant in documenting the emergence of specifically out gay cultures. Lucas Hilderbrand makes the case powerfully:

> Looking back on gay print culture and cinema, I have come to recognize that pornography constitutes much of if not *the* dominant content of gay visual culture of the 1970s and arguably beyond. Pornography was the *mainstream* of gay popular culture at one time, and

it has arguably remained its most prolific form [...]
gay pornography was even more centrally part of the
emergence – nay, explosion – of gay male public culture
and media in the immediate postliberation moment
(327-328).

The centrality of sexual representation to the emergence and
development of post liberation gay culture and identities would
be difficult to exaggerate. The complexity, and generativity, of
the relationship existing between gay spectators and images is
well characterized by Thomas Waugh when he writes that such
images "[provide] two points of entry for the gay spectator:
a site for identification with the narrative subject, and a site
for specular erotic pleasure in his object" ("Third Body" 144).
Moreover, the simultaneity of identification and pleasure
creates a dynamic for gay spectators with psychic and social
ramifications on the emergence of sexual subcultures such as
the barebackers discussed earlier and the gay male leather
community's adoption of looks and identities represented in
the work of artists like Tom of Finland. This spectatorship/
social context is essential in assessing the work of Peter Berlin
who adopted elements and visual conventions from the work
of other artists such as Tom for his own because as Muñoz has
aptly noted regarding the impact of such charged images,"
art conveys, translates, and engenders structures of feelings
– tropes of emotion and lived experience that are material
without necessarily being 'solid'" ("Ephemera" 10).
    Berlin starred in (and directed or co-directed) two feature
films as well as a handful of shorts and created a substantial

body of photographic work. Regardless of medium, the work always focusses on a carefully constructed and hypersexualized image of Berlin himself. This self-presentation consciously used clothing, accessories and even posture to maximize the artist's visual and erotic impact; boots, extremely tight trousers and abbreviated shirts, most often made – or customized – by Berlin as a kind of wearable art, were central to this self-presentation as was his signature "pageboy" hair style (Figure 3). So striking was his image that it compelled attention; John Waters points to this in the documentary *That Man: Peter Berlin* when he says of the over-the-top presentation that "I didn't know if he was a turn-on to me, but I couldn't stop looking" and it is to the question of the gaze and of looking that one must turn in order to come to grips with the power of Berlin's images.

Lucas Hilderbrand makes two important points regarding Berlin's first feature film, *Nights in Black Leather,* when he writes "[t]he film is narrated as a series of flashbacks as Berlin writes a letter to a friend back home in Germany, yet Peter shows little interiority. Everything about him – in the film – is about surfaces and appearances" (339). First, the emphasis the film gives to account by being framed as memories being put down in writing highlights the extent to which the film deploys language – puts literary strategies and ambitions to work. As filmmaker Wakefield Poole notes in the *That Man* documentary, Berlin's films often use voice-over to create continuity in visual representations that are frequently only tenuously narrative given their primary concern with the image of Berlin. The spoken text creates context and connections and draws attention to the affective or erotic charge of the image in highly-self-conscious

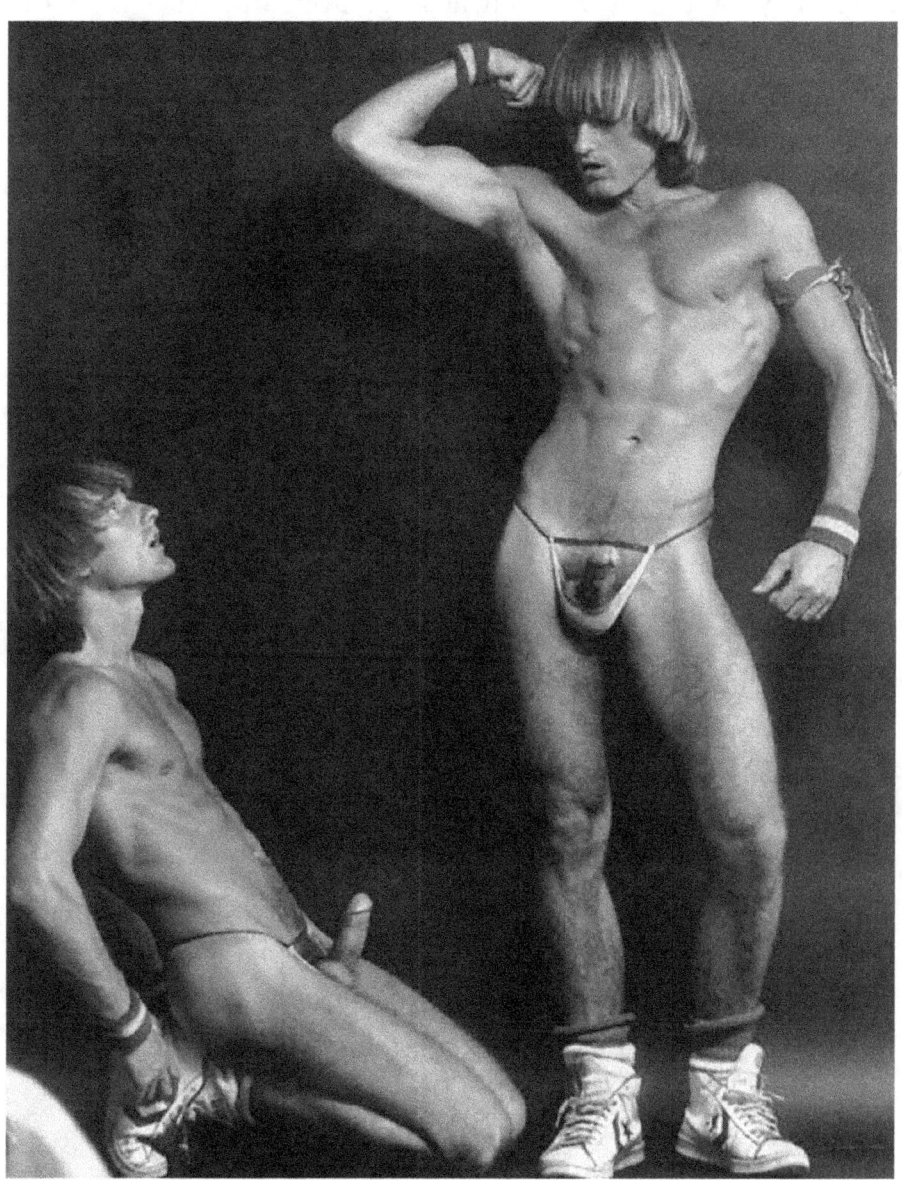

Figure 3. *Untitled*, double exposure photo, Peter Berlin, (1970s)

ways. Second, Hilderbrand suggests a dichotomy between interiority or depth and surfaces or appearances which the film itself may well be working to overturn through the intense focus they give to the feeling or sensation of looking and being looked at: the charge of observation as *aesthesis*, of approaching the world through sensory data (and, in this context through desire and sexual feeling specifically). Berlin himself has acknowledged the importance of such a practice of aesthesis for his experience of the erotic; in an interview with Canadian filmmaker Bruce LaBruce he says:

> [...] its not just that I get off by being watched, it's how someone is watching, who is watching, and what the person is doing. It's a two-way street [...] the whole visual thing is a big part of my sexuality. What is better than orgasm is the hours, the hours to get there [....] if you can stay in that state of being close to cumming – I have stayed in the state for 12, 20, 24 hours. Yes! A constant hard-on, a constant state of excitement. That is what good sex is [...]" (125).

Here the prospect of existing in a state of arousal for extended periods of time, of feeling one's existence as an operation of desire echoes something of Molinier's turbulent and erotic painted universe – suggesting its largest possibilities, perceptual and psychic. Moreover – even if one sets aside Berlin's personal feelings, or even intent – the film goes to great lengths to foreground the power of the erotically-charged gaze. *Nights in Black Leather* opens with a montage of Berlin walking through the streets of San Francisco in which the camera, standing in for the viewer's gaze, focusses first on one part of the star's body, his groin or his ass wrapped in tight black leather, or his bare chest, in a tight close-up. It lingers, then moves on to another part. Moreover, in addition to the insistent concern with directing the gaze fetishistically, the sequence is intercut with black and white still images of Berlin as if to insist on the image *as image* and not as merely a documentary record of someone walking. The naturalizable act of walking is instead visually reconfigured as a sequential series of pictures in which one can find erotic power and pleasure. The viewer is asked, and encouraged, to enjoy his or her gaze.

Later in the film the scopophilic imperative is given even greater emphasis in a sequence in which Berlin and a long-haired young man in a leather jacket cruise each other from across a street; exchanging glances, moving closer together, then away from each other, each positioning his body for the other's gaze, then looking again. The camera gives great importance to first one man's gaze and then the other while the voice-over narration elaborates on the feelings aroused through the cruising, describing the longing, the sense of arousal, the feeling of connection created simply by visual stimuli. The sequence is continued at some length: a length greater than any purely diegetic necessity. Each cut to a pair of eyes underlines the power of desiring someone and finding that desire reciprocated in a visual articulation of Lacan's dictum that it is "at the level of the desire of the Other that man can recognize his desire" (*Concepts*, 235). Thus, it is only possible to truly read the film's focus on the visual as lacking in interiority if one doesn't accept aesthesis as a way of knowing, or affect as a kind knowledge, which is clearly not the case within the filmic universe of *Nights in Black Leather.*

The power of "wanting" and "being wanted" is the animating motif in Berlin's work across its range. Both his 1973 short film *Waldeslust* and his 1976 short *Blueboys* include intensely voyeuristic scenes. In *Waldeslust,* Berlin and a young man encounter each other in a cruisey park and spend long minutes gazing at each other from behind bushes as they caress themselves. *Blueboys* takes the trope even further and heightens the charge by having two men watch each other – they are in the same house (and the same room) – through the glass panels in a door. Moreover, the square glass panels in the door form a kind of frame or lens, further emphasizing the power of the gaze. In this case the observation is made more deliberate through the addition of an artificial barrier that either man could eliminate if he cared to, but neither does, and that creates a sort of framed image merely by its position. In all these scenes the act of looking is given primary attention, not simply as a physical action, but as an epistemological one – as the vehicle of the desire to see and to know, as the bearer of the weight of desire and as a connection to another human being.

That charge is also present in Berlin's photographic work, and in ways through which a parallel might be drawn with the self-representations of Molinier. Like Molinier, Berlin's work is profoundly concerned with transformation, with the remaking of the self into an erotic image or icon, with heightening desire and desirability; it is through the use of costuming, posture, gesture and positioning that the artist creates a character called

"Peter Berlin" whose appearance seems to transcend ordinary manhood. This "more than human" quality was characterized by Jack Wrangler, another porn icon of the 1970s, as taking "an erotic fantasy and [stylizing] it, almost like a choreographer with a ballet dancer" and as a, significantly, "surrealistic dream" (*That Man*). The reference to the "surreal" here testifies to the extent to which Berlin, like surrealist artists, was in pursuit of some unreachable horizon in his work, not with himself simply as a person, a man, but of some absolutely sexual version of himself. The self-portraits, even when more conventional, are always concerned with their "viewability" – with sightlines, angles and the effect of light on oiled skin, and clinging fabric – in ways that allow for what Williams characterizes as the "distance or gap between subject and object [needed] for desire to come into play" (193). In a series of double exposures (Figure 3 and Figure 4), however, Berlin joins this superhuman quality with the dialectic of look and response so central to the films. In these photographs he captures his own image twice: in different positions and different attire but always positioned in relation to one another. Thus, one can see him as two leather-clad bikers revealing themselves to each other and succumbing, or as young athletes coming together, or as street toughs posing for each other's pleasure. In these photographs the pleasures of the gaze and its capacity to generate subtle threads of attraction and energy are both represented and interpellated, suggested in the relationship between the identical imaged bodies and stirred up in the viewer simultaneously, and thus operating textually and socially with equal force. Here, as in Molinier's self-representation, the same figure and the same body

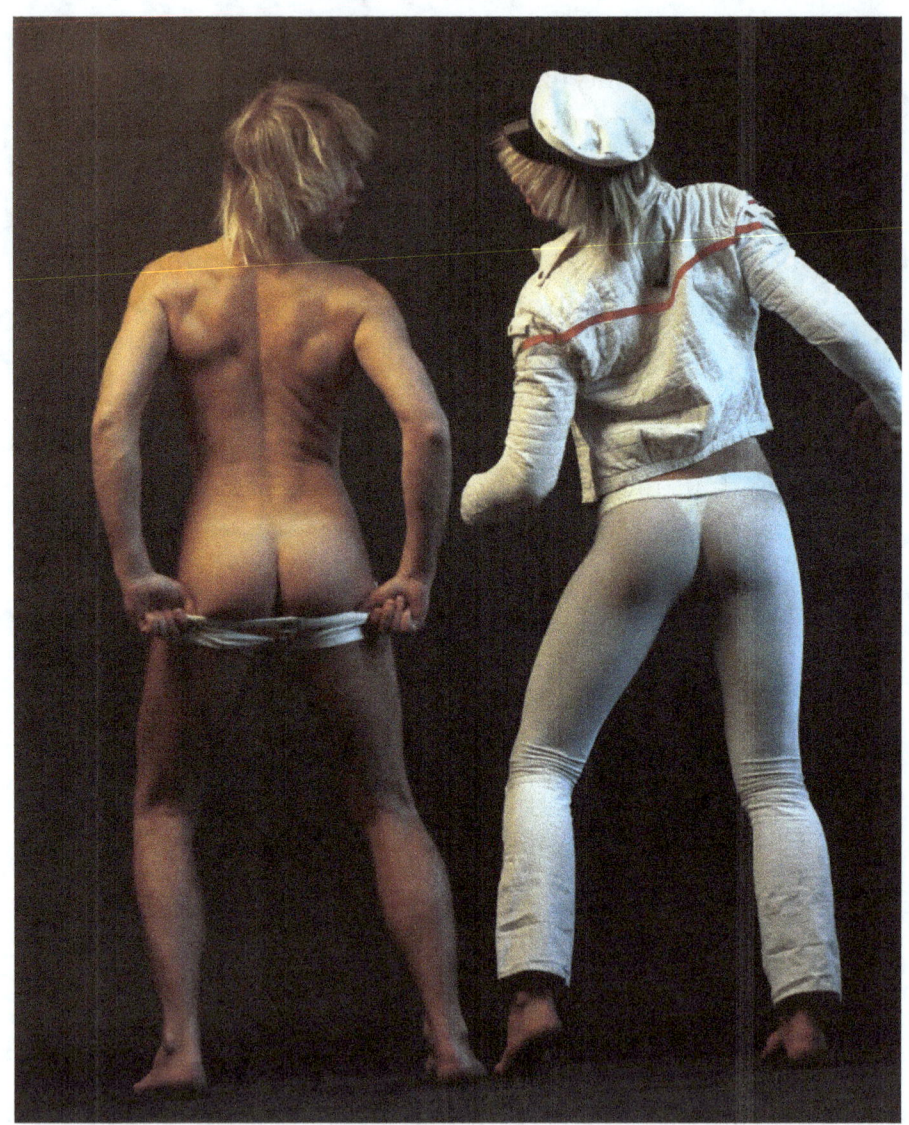

Figure 4. *Untitled*, double exposure photo, Peter Berlin, (1970s)

transforms and proliferates; it acts as document and index of the force of desire as a power one projects into the world, and a quest for the imagined horizon in which it might – theoretically – become actualized.

Hilderbrand comments on this in his analysis of the archive of 1970s gay erotic cinema, observing,

This sense of search and projection pervades the 1970s gay erotic films. I have been struck by the possibility for experimentation in their form and even more so that their recurring narrative conceits are structured as memories, daydreams, period pieces, and drug altered consciousness [...] early feature-length gay films repeatedly and explicitly foreground nostalgia and fantasy, not realism or diegetic 'actuality,' as their primary narrative logics. Such recurrent strategies both suggest continuities with avant-garde queer cinema of the previous decade (such as the films of Kenneth Anger, Jack Smith, Steven Arnold, and even Pat Rocco) and the search for ways to express as specifically gay consciousness and history [...] (344)

The utopian aspect of Berlin's apparent narcissism lies in precisely the complex tension of seeking the erotic and projecting it outwards to render it perceptible to others, the understanding of desire as a force and a project: in his cinema and photographic work Peter Berlin is not simply indulging himself, he is reaching for – and failing to achieve, all too often – some sensed ideal, some fabulous place or thing – that utopian horizon, once again. And I would argue that this ties it not simply to a queer avant-garde as Hilderbrand notes, but to the historical avant-garde more broadly, including surrealism, a connection well established in Waugh's groundbreaking archaeology in which he includes "art" (including experimental and avant-garde traditions) among the four basic classificatory "regimes" of gay male erotic images he identifies (*Imagine*, 59-175). Moreover, it links the project to other practices with ties to avant-garde activities, notably the subject of the next probe: the esoteric.

CHAPTER 4
ESOTERICISM

The extended field of the esoteric, comprised of such things as mediumism, paranormal phenomena, divination, alchemy, witchcraft, ceremonial magic, and visionary or mystical experience is a foundational strand in the fabric of surrealism; it is also one that has attracted increasing critical interest among scholars who trace particular aspects of such interest and attempt to elaborate what sort of significance the occult had within surrealist practice. Tessel M. Bauduin's 2014 book, *Surrealism and the Occult* seeks to respond to two common critical positions on the matter: one that see occult ideas as marginal to surrealism and the other that maintains occultism is a central, even determinant focus of the movement. Bauduin, opposing these dichotomous positions, argues that occultism is a continuous but not dominant presence in the theory and practice of surrealism: "a process much more concerned with making surrealism complex and multi-layered, and magical in the meaning of pre-rational in its rapport with the world, rather than with making it an occult movement," (194). This probe shall attempt to build on that assessment by investigating, not how important or unimportant the esoteric is to surrealism, but rather *what kind of role* it plays, in what ways it serves the ends

Bauduin identifies, of adding complexity and magic to the surrealist project; not so much how much esotericism there is in the movement, but what such esotericism actually does for it.

The occult is also a conspicuous presence within gay liberation and queer political and cultural life as well, one driving a variety of subcultures and identity formations within the movement(s) and animating many of its canonical texts and films; we will turn our attention to these in due course. However, before analyzing specific works it will prove useful to consider a critical formulation with much use in evaluating the role of the esoteric in both surrealism and queerness.

In recent years the recuperations of esotericism by popular culture have been theorized as "occulture" by a number of thinkers, most notably the scholar of religion Christopher Partridge who characterized the subcultural forms emerging around and deploying a broad range of mystical and spiritual ideas with the term while stressing the practical, lived nature of the matrix of ideas and images so designated as "not a worldview, but [...] a resource on which people draw, a reservoir of ideas, beliefs, practices, and symbols" (84). One should note, that although the term has gained a certain currency and although Partridge is often cited as its source, the word "occulture" is almost certainly a coinage of musician and artist Genesis Breyer P-Orridge, a fact acknowledged by Partridge himself (68). Questions of attribution aside, the term has been taken up because it provides a useful theoretical tool that emphasizes "the constructed discursive nature of concepts such 'as 'religion,' the 'spiritual' and 'the secular' " (Kokkinen, 9) and I would add the "occult" itself, and it enables one to "take into account the nature of these concepts as manufactured categories, which people (including scholars) utilize as discursive strategies and ideologies" (14). The word thus allows for a discussion of occult ideas and practices as *creative* and *experiential* in nature while putting aside other questions (such as their "truth," "reality" or "efficacity") which – although interesting in themselves – are not always pertinent in assessing how the ideas circulate, are conceived of, or actually operate in people's lives and communities. It allows for a focus on what people *do* with occult ideas and practices, rather than what they *are* in and of themselves. Occulture is a more fluid concept than magic because it is "never ever occultism *per se* or culture *per se*, but always [consists] of interchangeability" (Abrahamsson,11), and if this discursive flexibility makes it valuable for assessing the place of the esoteric in surrealism and gay liberation, it can also be joined with the formulations of other thinkers that provide a means for assessing some of the *specific* forms it takes in the thought and works of the movements.

Andreas Kilcher's "Seven Epistemological Theses on Esotericism" offer another theoretical tool for parsing some of the fluid operations of occulture and its reservoir of ideas, beliefs, and symbols; his second, fifth, and sixth theses have specific import in this regard. Thesis 2 affirms that esotericism may be grasped by "means of a *praxiological* concept of knowledge [....] knowledge as performance, as culture" (144) while Thesis 5 holds that the "epistemology of esotericism stands in a dialectical relation not only to scientific knowledge, but also to religious belief [....] esotericism emerges as a hybrid formation: as a speculative knowledge" (146), and the gap between these assertions provides a generative space for considering the possible role of esotericism for a Queer Surrealism. The double emphasis on praxis and performance is fundamental since both surrealists and gay liberationists are concerned with the "arts of living" or the overlap of creative practice with and as constitutive of daily life with the elision of the line between art and life as we have seen in the discussion of the role of eros and of automatism and self-representation in their work. The rites and writings of the esoteric expand on the possibilities of such practices and create the opportunity for greater epistemological range and adventure. Kilcher's sixth thesis leavens these possibilities with an explicit linking of esotericism, creative practice, and utopia by stating that esotericism "brings knowledge to the very boundaries of myth and literature. It is not built primarily on logical-rational foundations or empirical proof, but on narrative, imaginal, aesthetic construction, which can be qualified as speculative, idealistic, utopian or fantastic according to one's perspective" (147). Thus, esotericism may operate as an expansion of the forms and techniques for knowing and moving through the world that enables the constant repositioning of the utopian horizons of the surreal and the queer while ensuring they maintain compelling discursive and imaginal forms, forms given to them by the stories and histories of living queers and surrealists, stories and histories it is our preoccupation to unpack here.

THE QUESTION OF OCCULTATION

In *The Second Manifesto of Surrealism* (1929) Breton takes stock of the movement he helped found, assesses the results of its activities and developments within its ranks since the publication of its first official public declaration five years earlier. He also looks towards the movement's future and calls for a new direction in carefully chosen terms: he "[ASKS] FOR THE PROFOUND, THE VERITABLE OCCULTATION OF SURREALISM" (*Manifestoes*, 178, upper case in the original).[50] The choice of the word "occultation" is a curious one and has prompted much discussion given its various denotations; it suggests both hidden from view and immersed in the esoteric. However, in the context of the larger text it becomes clear that it is meant in expansive, and plural, senses and that Breton's "call for occultation was twofold: he wished to obstruct the deformation of the ideas conveyed by surrealism because of the publicity it was receiving at the time; he also [...] was obviously referring to the so-called 'occult-sciences', a term used at the beginning of the twentieth century interchangeably with both occultism and esotericism" (Ferentinou, 105). Both these senses were vital to Breton in repositioning the movement; withdrawing or concealing surrealism from the public gaze seemed necessary in order to protect the movement's oppositional position to the larger culture, especially in the context of its volatile relationship with French communism, and a renewed focus on the occult constituted a return to one

---

50 "JE DEMANDE L'OCCULTATION PROFONDE, VERITABLE DU SURRÉALISME" (*Second manifeste*, 128)

of the movements key sources; surrealism, after all, begins with an interest in trance states and mediumism, automatic writing, and alchemy among other occult practices.

Surrealist interest in the esoteric is widespread and prominent; a large variety of texts and works investigating such ideas far in excess of the *Second Manifesto* – with its call for occultation and invocation of the great alchemist Nicholas Flamel – would be created by members of the movement. The painter Kurt Seligmann, for example, would publish a weighty history of the occult in the conclusion of which he articulates a particularly surrealist understanding of the significance of magic: "Magic was a stimulus to thinking. It freed man from fears, endowed him with a feeling of his power to control the world, sharpened his capacity to imagine, and kept alive his dreams of higher achievement" (483). Such a list of functions neatly parallels the central surrealist concerns of freedom, imagination, and dreams while underlining the way the movement's interest in various forms of occultism is often essentially epistemological. Moreover, one should recall that the movement's roots lie in an idiosyncratic confluence of psychoanalysis, a particularly revolutionary strain of Romanticism, and mediumship. In its earliest days, while many founding members were still active in Dada and the first *Manifesto*, which explicitly declares the secrets of surrealist composition are "magical" (29), was yet to be published, the group held a series of experiments with trance states that would have a determinant impact on the emergence of surrealism as a self-defined and autonomous entity. The period is documented in Louis Aragon's *A Wave of Dreams* and two essays by Breton: "The Mediums Enter" published in 1922 and "A Letter to Seers" which appears in1925 the year following the *Manifesto,* and in which he addresses mediums of as "the only tributaries and the only guardians of the Secret. I am speaking of the Great Secret, of the Unrevealable" (197)[51]. The emphasis given to trance states, which are clearly linked to the practice of automatism, underlines the extent to which even in its early years the movement is conscious of the connections between its diverse sources and the instrumental value of the techniques it appropriates from them. Thompson, for example, points out the importance surrealists found in mediumship when she writes that

"automativity functioned as [a] radical authorial/corporeal/political/semiotic practice" (2) that allowed "radical politics [to] be smuggled into public discourse under the aegis of supernatural possession" (3), suggesting again that surrealist interest in occultism is practical and conceived of as consubstantial with its creative and political activities, that it is occultural in precisely the way Kokkinen points out.

Morrison writes of the visual and textual production of mid-twentieth century artist Ithell Colquhoun, a particularly resonant case study, as a bridge between British and/or international Surrealism and the contemporaneous occult revival. His article is effective in making the historical and

51   "seules tributaires et seules gardiennes du Secret. Je parle du grand Secret, de l'Indérobable." (*Lettre aux voyantes*, np, the text appears on page 20 of the facsimile reproduction of *La Révolution Surréaliste*, Number 5)

intellectual links between the movements clear and offers a convincing case for Colquhoun and her work as a locus of overlap and synthesis of diverse strands of thought. Morrison also examines the way in which that linkage suggests an emerging understanding of automatism "not simply as an aesthetic or even purely psychological exploration but as an epistemological practice" (588), an observation that clearly points towards the ways in which the practice, in its cultivation of trance states, not only creates new objects of knowledge but seeks to extend the reach of consciousness to other subjects, and the material world: an expansion with clear social and political import.

At the heart of Morrison's argument is his reading of Colquhoun's novel *The Goose of Hermogenes* which is steeped in gothic ambiance and structured in twelve chapters corresponding to the twelve steps of the alchemical process[52] required to create the philosopher's stone – from calcination to projection (606). The plot of the novel, Colquhoun's only published extended fiction until the posthumous appearance of *I Saw Water* in 2014 , follows the first-person narrative of a woman who goes to visit a sinister and reclusive uncle residing on a volcanic island situated either in the Azores or on Corsica. The plot involves demonic possession, psychic visions and a town populated by the dead. Despite the deliberateness of such a structure and a narrative rooted in generic conventions, the book was "largely produced by automatic processes (mostly from dream material) and put into a self-consciously alchemical

52 The most recent edition contains an additional chapter titled "hexen-tanz".

framework" (605) and pushes its development forward largely through the use of a pattern of esoteric symbols. The dominant scenes and settings in the novel are often spaces of liminality and the blurring of duality which dramatize, as it were, the alchemical union of opposites. Moreover, in 1955 the author undertook a series of illustrations to accompany the novel which remained unpublished until 2018. Thus *The Goose of Hermogenes* both represents and embodies a series of harmonized or conjoined oppositions: visual and literary representation, automatic composition and conscious structure, finished and incomplete form, prominent among them. The deliberate embodiment of dialectical tensions and the way they call out to the reader or viewer to engage, to create their resolution through the reading process demonstrates the use of surrealist technologies for epistemological ends, or the "production of sources of knowledge" (587), specifically, in Morrison's analysis, ones aimed at "a transpersonal epistemology – a crossing of barriers between individual minds, and between time and place" (588) which is to say, in many ways, towards the creation of community and a transformed relationship to reality.

The importance accorded to occultural ideas and practices by key figures within the surrealist movement is powerfully illustrated by their preoccupations during the war years. A number of surrealists, and affiliated artists and intellectuals, including Breton and his family spent part of 1940 at the Villa Air-Bel in Marseille while they worked to secure safe passage out of Europe and away from the war (Polizzotti 485 - 496). During this time a group came together to work on a new deck of cards which has come to be known by a number of names (*The Surrealist Tarot*, and *The Marseille Game* among them) but which shall be referred to here as *The Marseille Deck*. The Deck saw a transformation of the suits into "Love," graphically represented as a flame, "Dream," a black star, "Revolution," a bloody wheel, and "Knowledge," a lock. The Court Cards became the Genius (King), Mermaid (Queen) and Magus (Jack). Moreover, the court cards were represented as figures from the surrealist pantheon of ancestors, thus the Genius of Flames was Baudelaire, the Mermaid of Stars, Alice (from *Alice in Wonderland*), and the Magus of Locks, significantly enough was Paracelsus, the late medieval alchemist (Breton, "Deck," 49). The inclusion of a "magus" and figures like Paracelsus immediately incline one to view the revamped deck as a form of the tarot, especially since one of the best-known of the tarot decks is also named for Marseilles, and the surrealists would certainly have had an awareness of the various tarot decks. However, Breton's short text explicitly ties the deck to playing cards and stresses its suitability "for all the traditional games" (49).[53] Thus, the Marseilles Deck operates in a way that blurs the distinction between playing cards and divination, particularly in light of the importance the surrealists ascribe to the playing of games – a regular feature of their daily café gatherings – and the manner in which they were understood to be a way of provoking revelations and new understandings. For the surrealists games are "[b]ased on the pooling of mental resources and the chance associations of words or images, games deliberately break with the normal flow of discourse

53   "tous les jeux anciens" (*Jeu de Marseilles*, 68)

which threatens to release clichés [...] by producing singular analogies and unprecedented associations" (Adamowicz, 55). The full significance of games such as "the exquisite corpse" then lies in their power to "[push] analogy to the limit" (82) since for Breton "Poetic analogy has this in common with mystical analogy: it [...] let[s] the mind apprehend the interdependence of two objects of thought located on different planes" (*Ascendant Sign*, 105).[54] Hence, any game played with the newly invented cards would necessarily aim to unveil the unknown in a way that, at the very least, is analogous to fortune telling.

BRETON, ARCANUM 17 & THE MYSTERY OF THE WORLD

However, although surrealism's interest in occulture begins with mediumship and fortune telling it extends across the whole breadth and depth of the field, encompassing mythology, alchemy, and mysticism or visionary experience as well. Breton's *Arcanum 17* is an example of that range, though it too has roots in the rich symbolism of the tarot. The work, emblematic of the movement's growing public interest in the occult in the war years, was written during Breton's exile in North America and while on a trip to the Gaspésie, and represents a further development of some of the ideas and techniques he began exploring in his earlier long form prose writing (the specifics of the form are idiosyncratic and difficult to pin down in generic terms) *Mad Love* and *Nadja*. Like those earlier works, *Arcanum*

54   "L'analogie poétique a ceci de commun avec l'analogie mystique qu'elle [...] faire appréhender à l'esprit l'interdépendance de deux objets de pensée situés sur des plans différents" (*Signe ascendant*, 134)

17 explores the encounter with the world and the affective charge of perception in deep phenomenological detail; unlike them, however, the experience unfolded in this book is not that of an urban environment, but rather the encounter with nature. The book constitutes a noteworthy extension of surrealism's long interest in the phenomenology of experience and focuses on a powerful vision in which loss, displacement and the weight of history meet a call for renewal, all filtered through a sensory and intellectual apparatus that fuses the romantic with the Romantic. Surrealism's inheritance from Romanticism is well-established and was acknowledged by Breton in his lecture "What is Surrealism" in which he writes regarding the connection: "Romanticism – of which we are quite ready to appear historically today as the tail, though in that case an *excessively prehensile tail*" (132, emphasis Breton's).[55] In *Arcanum 17* however this intellectual and poetic debt takes on greater visibility and importance.

The book opens with a meditation on Percé Rock and the bird colonies on Bonaventure Island that very rapidly moves from observation of the physical characteristics of the island itself to a consideration of the political situation in Europe, and then to a deeply moving declaration of love. In beginning, Breton writes,

> I was immediately taken with the extravagant character of the whole inscription. The word symphony has been used with regard to the rock ensemble that dominates

---

55 "ce romantisme dont nous voulons bien, historiquement, passer aujourd'hui pour la queue, *mais alors la queue tellement préhensile*" (*Qu'est-ce que le surréalisme*, 22)

Percé, but here was an image which only became powerful from the moment one discovered that the repose of the birds was a perfect match for the craggy shapes of those sheer battlements, so that the organic rhythm was perfectly superimposed on the inorganic rhythm, as if it needed to fuse with it in order to hold itself together. Who could have thought of lending the elasticity of wings to an avalanche? The different rock beds, slipping with one supple line from the horizontal to the oblique at a forty-five degree angle to the water, are delineated by a marvelous chalk mark, constantly agitated (I'm daydreaming of a turned-down bedspread of the same color white, in fine lace whose large flowers fascinated me on waking when I was a child. (26)[56]

This early passage presages much that will dominate the book and mark its tone; one sees the absolute interpenetration of subjectivity and world so characteristic of surrealism. The inanimate is given meaning by the mobility of the birds occupying it, and they "fuse with it." The landscape enters the

56 "mais j'étais aussitôt repris par le caractère de toute l'inscription. On a pu parler de symphonie à propos de l'ensemble rocheux qui domine Percé, mais c'est là une image qui ne prend de force qu'à partir de l'instant où l'on découvre que le repos des oiseaux épouse les anfractuosités de cette muraille à pic, en sorte que le rythme organique se superpose ici de justesse au rythme inorganique comme s'il avait besoin de se consolider sur lui pour s'entretenir. Qui se fût avisé de prêter le ressort des ailes à l'avalanche! Les différents lits de pierre, d'un ligne souple glissant de l'horizontale à l'oblique à quarante-cinq degrés sur la mer, sont décrits d'un merveilleux trait de craie en constante ébullition (je songe au dessus de lit replié, de même blancheur, en dentelle au filet, dont les grands fleurs me fascinaient au réveil quant j'étais enfant." (*Arcane 17*, 6-7).

psyche of the poet as both itself and in the form of a childhood memory; avalanches are elastic, chalk becomes animated. Such leaps of association and consciousness become, moreover, more common and more extreme in the pages to follow. Breton perceives the flapping of flags on the boat on which he and Elisa (his wife, Elisa Breton, *née* Elisa Bindhoff Enet) are travelling against the memory of the red banners marking construction projects in Paris (in one of which he sees the letters S.A.D.E., significantly enough given Sade's prominence as a forebear of the movement) and the black flags of an anarchist demonstration from his youth (30-31).[57] The boundaries between the present and the past, the natural world and the human, ideas and objects blur and blend in these passages in ways consistent with the declarations of both the *Manifesto* regarding the resolution of binaries and Gellman's claims in the *Stanford Encyclopedia of Philosophy* online that mystical experience is a "unitive experience [that] involves a phenomenological de-emphasis, blurring, or eradication of multiplicity, where the cognitive significance of the experience is deemed to lie precisely in that phenomenological feature" (np). Furthermore, the occasion for the text – the contemplation of a landscape – calls to mind the prominent tradition of "nature mysticism" which the *Encyclopedia* characterizes as "extrovertive," a "mystical consciousness of the unity of nature overlaid onto one's sense perception of the world [...] as when experiencing God's presence when gazing at a snowflake" (np). This is a tradition long associated with poets, particularly the Romantics, whose writing is marked by "a sense of of the immanence of the One

---

57   The passage appears on pp 13-14 in the French edition.

or God or soul in Nature" (Bishop, 13). Thus, *Arcanum 17* opens with a vision of the sort well-established in poetic tradition, but ramps up rapidly, becoming more intense and more charged in form and content. Two of *Arcanum 17's* set pieces, the meditation on the figure of Melusina and another on that of the tarot card "The Star," the seventeenth card of the Major Arcana which gives the book its title, are especially relevant in demonstrating the particularities of the surrealist vision and the manners in which it is marked by a sense of psychospiritual continuity.

Breton's preferred version of the Melusina legend is that in which she is the protector of the Chateau of Lusignan, and he conjures her into his text using a number of highly-charged invocations: "Melusina no longer under the burden of the fate unleashed on her by man alone, Melusina rescued. Melusina before the scream that will announce her return [...] like the stone of the Apocalypse and like all things" (*Arcanum*, 63)[58] and "Melusina with lower joints of broken stones or aquatic plants or the down of a nest, she's the one I invoke, she's the only one I can see who could redeem this savage epoch" (63).[59] Of note in these lines is the manner in which the image of Melusina combines a surprising range of substances, moving from the mineral kingdom to that of plants in order to suggest the underlying unity of the natural world. She becomes, as Bauduin remarks in her study of the occult influences on

58 Mélusine non plus sous le poids de la fatalité déchaînée sur elle par l'homme seul, Mélusine délivrée, Mélusine avant le cri qui doit annoncer son retour [...] comme la pierre de l'Apocalypse et comme toutes choses" (Ibid, 65-66).
59 "Mélusine aux attaches inférieures de pierraille ou d'herbes aqua-tiques ou de duvet de nid, c'est elle que j'invoque, je ne vois qu'elle qui puisse rédimer cette époque sauvage," (Ibid, 65).

Surrealism, "Nature embodied, an undine or elemental spirit of water," (*Occult*, 150) a particularly appropriate incarnating symbol for a vision revealed shipboard. Assuming the function of presiding goddess in this text, Melusina marks an important moment in the attempt at "the construction of a 'collective mythology' which the surrealists pursued from the late 1930s and particularly from the 1940s onward" (Ferentinou 106). Beyond that, however, through the blending of separate objects into one all-encompassing potency, she is also figured in ways linking her to the movement of history through the poet's reference to "return" and her power to redeem a savage epoch. As Hollenback states is inherent in much mystical experience (40 - 41), this assertion is both metaphorical and literal for Breton; he further insists that artists and intellectuals must "bring man down from a position of power, which, it has been sufficiently demonstrated, he has misused [and] restore this power to the hands of woman" (Breton, *Arcanum* 62).[60] Moreover, however troubling the invocation of the "child woman" that follows this vision is – "by definition a reductive designation even though he means only the highest compliment by it" (Conley, *Automatic* 123) – the fact remains that in a text written in 1944 and against the backdrop of World War II, such statements remain imbued with significant proto-feminist sentiment, and Breton, however much a product of his staggeringly patriarchal times, intuits here something of the most dangerous implications of his epoch's structures of gender/power. And, as Conley states "by acknowledging his own inability to comprehend women fully,

60   "déchoir l'homme d'un pouvoir dont il est suffisamment établi qu'il a mésusé, pour remettre ce pouvoir entre les mains de la femme," (Ibid, 64).

and by praising them [...] Breton was establishing a space for women to claim as their own within avant-garde thinking in the twentieth century" (124).

Similar import can be found in the vision of the "Star" card, which is at the heart of the book. An iconic image in the world of the occult, this card bears – in the version found in the "Tarot of Marseilles," the deck most likely to be familiar to Breton – the image of a woman, nude and kneeling by a pond below a sky filled with seven stars. She pours out two urns of water, one of which flows onto the land in five rivulets, while the other spills into the water of the pond. The card's traditional meanings are associated with hope, renewal and inspiration and in Breton's hands it becomes the occasion for a meditation on the War, its impact and possible outcomes.

The vision begins with the apparition of seven flowers that transform into stars above the woman emptying out her vessels (who is identified with both the serpent woman and Eve by the poet), after which Breton hears the voices of the "two streams." The "left-hand stream" says it "burn[s] and rouse[s] [...] [it] can't help but cause the destruction of all living things [being] devoted only to what threatens to fall lethargically to the earth's surface. [It] is headed for that bleak pond where under phosphorescent creams, ideas which have ceased to move men come to be buried. And this pond belongs to the dogmas that have met their end" (75-76).[61] The right-hand stream, contrarily,

61   "Je brûle et je réveille [...] je ne pourrais que causer la perte de tout qui vit, je ne me dois qu'à ce qui menace de tomber en léthargie à la surface de la terre. C'est à ce morne étang que je vais, où, sous des crèmes phosphorescentes, les idées viennent s'ensevelir dès qu'elles on cessé de mouvoir l'homme. Et cet étang est celui des dogmes qui ont pris fin," (Ibid, 86)

speaks thus: "I bewitch, and I multiply [...] and I'm heading for the earth which loves me, for the earth which couldn't fulfill the seed's promise without me [...] And ideas would also cease to be fertile [...]" (76).[62] Given how these passages follow directly on a consideration of the political situation in France, the vision of the two streams is resonant with a palpable sense of Breton's belief that history has arrived at a turning point and is faced with two radically divergent possibilities: renewal or collapse. The vision is, however, complex and mobile; the super-sensory confusion of the various elements begins with the window in which the entire visionary spectacle unveils – which may be prompted by an actual window on the vessel on which Breton is travelling – and grows more vehement, more fantastic, as it unfolds, blending fire and water with cream and ideas in one stream and fertility, magic, and the earth in the other. Here two of the principal qualities of the mystical experience noted by Hollenback are evident: the blending of the literal and metaphorical and the historical conditioning of a fundamentally "amorphous" content (41). Though the specific features of Breton's vision are highly imaged, they are occultural in the strict sense, clearly meant to be discursive and political forces *in the world* and are rooted in the need to confront the massive destruction wrought by War. Moreover, the poet's sense of urgency, manifest as fear on one hand, or stream and hope on the other, is mitigated by the optimism of the articulation with its magical transformations, which echo the "soteriological content" also remarked on by Hollenback

62   "J'enchante et je multiplie [...] et je vais à la terre qui m'aime, à la terre qui sans moi ne pourrait remplir les promesses de la graine [...] Et les idées cesseraient aussi d'être fécondes," (Ibid, 87)

(40) as another recurring feature of much canonical mystical experience. This is particularly the case as the optimism, or sense of possible renewal, is rooted in the very continuity of existence that is the substance of the vision: the oneness of rock and birds, water and sky, the fact that it is a single person that pours out the two streams.

Also important in any unpacking of the text is the poet's relationship with his wife which runs through the account as a companion to the visionary content and "heavily ladens" the experience with "affect," to paraphrase yet another defining feature identified in the literature on mysticism even as it recalls the importance of eros in surrealism. At irregular intervals the author inserts his thoughts and feelings regarding his companion into the primary flow of events in *Arcanum 17*, as in this case near the beginning: "It will be a beautiful day, I see it filtering through your eyes where it began, cloudier, by being so beautiful" (39).[63] Here he suggests that the content of this work stems from his connection with his wife as its source. The trope of love returns frequently, sometimes blending the figure of an actual woman with those in the vision, as in these instances: "I love you because the sea air and the mountain air, mixed here in their original purity, are no more exempt from miasmas and no more intoxicating than the air of your soul" (40)[64] or "[w]hen fate brought you to me, an enormous shadow was in me and I might even say it was inside me that the

63 "La journée sera belle, je la vois se filtrer dans tes yeux où elle a commencé, plus trouble, par être si belle," (Ibid, 29)
64 "Et je t'aime parce que l'air de la mer et celui de la montagne, confondus ici dans leur pureté originelle, ne sont pas plus exempts de miasmes et plus enivrants que celui de ton âme," (Ibid, 31)

window opened. That revelation you brought me [...]" (68).[65] These observations are consistent, moreover, with Breton's earlier work; passionate romantic love constitutes the central thread uniting many of the poet's books – *Nadja* and *Mad Love* both prominently feature the author's love of a woman marked by "something enchanting and magical" (Bauduin, 149) and the unfolding of their relationship, but in *Arcanum 17*, the identification of a female lover with the magical power of the unveiled universe in the form of supernatural creatures such as fairies, witches, and Egyptian deities – Isis appears in the book – reaches its apex, both in terms of affect and metaphorical density. And, although there is an irreducible idealizing (and hence objectifying) quality to such transformations of an actual person into an image, any serious reading of the text must recall the extent to which Surrealist poetics assert the importance of analogical thinking which "let[s] the mind apprehend the interdependence of two objects of thought located on different planes" (Breton, *Ascendant Sign*,105).[66] A frank affirmation of different registers of meaning greatly mitigates the claims of any reductive reading of the equivalency, given that it acknowledges meaning or significance as relational rather than fixed. Moreover, as Katja Silverman observes, idealization is "at the heart of" love and rather than simply arguing against it, one might better "imagine new uses to which it might be put" (2) which is precisely what Breton is doing in this instance. And

65 "Quand le sort t'a portée à ma rencontre, la plus grande ombre était en moi et je puis dire que c'est en mois que cette fenêtre s'est ouverte. La révélation que tu m'apportais [...]" (Ibid, 74)
66 "faire appréhender à l'esprit l'interdépendance de deux objets de pensée situés sur des plans différents" (*Signe ascendant*, 134)

it is this evocation of love and desire that brings us to Bataille's very different, indeed singular, exploration of the the mystical valences of the erotic.

ABJECTION, ECSTASY AND MME. EDWARDA

In his hallucinatory erotic novella *Madame Edwarda*, Georges Bataille dramatizes some of his foundational ideas regarding the interface of visionary, or "inner experience," and the erotic. The book is the narrative of one encounter between the protagonist and the prostitute whose name provides the title. Strolling through Paris late one night the narrator is overcome with an uncanny sexualized malaise. He removes his trousers and continues to walk around the Tenth Arrondissement while aroused. Coming to his senses momentarily he puts his clothes back on and decides to go to a brothel. There he meets and has sex with Madame Edwarda who, during their encounter, tells him she is "God." Following this interlude, she puts on a mask and cloak and asks him to go out into the streets with her, which he does, and the pair share a strange and intense experience during which Edwarda appears to lose her mind. This brief synopsis, however, cannot convey the intensity of the book, nor the complex philosophical ambitions that drive the narrative and that underlie its curious construction and frequent apparent digressions.

Madame Edwarda's opening establishes its programme unambiguously. There is a block of text, nearly centred on an otherwise blank page, that appears unrelated to the narrative and which reads,

Anguish only is sovereign absolute. The sovereign is a king no more: it dwells low-hiding in big cities. It knits itself up in silence, obscuring its sorrow. Crouching thick-wrapped, there it waits, lies waiting for the advent of him who shall strike a general terror; but meanwhile and even so its sorrow scornfully mocks at all that comes to pass, at all there is.(147)[67]

This abstract and theoretical preamble, isolated and etched with reversions and near contradictions – "low-hiding" and "thick-wrapped," "sovereign absolute" and "king no more," "sorrow" and "mockery" – is followed immediately by the beginning of the narrative. It is very different in tone and noticeably more embodied and more abject, though also marked by the tension created by the deliberate opposition of various contradictory things. It opens with a depiction of the first-person narrator overcome with anguish that is bodily, that makes him want to vomit, as he spots two "furtive whores sneaking down the stair of a urinal" (148)[68]. After this sighting, the narrator, "Pierre Angélique," a name that on its own foreshadows the text's concern with the sacred (along with some of its very specific images), drinks himself into a state and is overcome by the desire to expose himself to "the night

67   The translation here is a free one. The original French reads, in all caps, thus: "MON ANGOISSE EST ENFIN L'ABSOLUE SOUVERAINE. MA SOUVERAINETÉ MORTE EST A LA RUE. INSAISISSABLE – AUTOUR D'ELLE UN SILENCE DE TOMBE – TAPIE DANS L'ATTENTE D'UN TERRIBLE – ET POURTANT SA TRISTESSE SE RIT DE TOUT" (*Madame Edwarda*, 327).
68   "deux filles furtives dans escalier d'un lavabo […]" (Ibid, 329)

there in those empty streets" (148)[69]. The juxtaposition of these passages at the beginning very clearly establishes the text's simultaneous operation on two distinct registers of writing; *Madame Edwarda* will operate diegetically and philosophically, it will be an erotic and a theoretical text at once.

The implicit promise of this pairing dominates the novella and constitutes its central theme: the consubstantiality of body and soul, the fundamental unity of squalor, pleasure and transcendence. One of the most compelling instances of this conjunction occurs when the narrator/protagonist visits a brothel called "The Mirrors," – whose name itself implies the meeting of the material and the intangible, body and image – and encounters the eponymous prostitute Madame Edwarda. As the drunken protagonist clasps the woman to him, he finds himself transported "as though [he were] borne aloft in a flight of headless and unbodied angels [...] until [he becomes] unhappy and [feels] forsaken, as one is when in the presence of GOD" (149)[70]. The near-simultaneity of ecstasy and despair, heightened by the manner in which the "angels" are described as headless or mutilated, suggests the extremity of the protagonist's state, its extension to the limit of experience, a theme central to another of Bataille's major works: *Inner Experience*. This bodily transport is given greater significance a few pages later when Madame Edwarda herself validates his experience in an exchange whose incoherence underlines the

---

69 "La nuit était nue dans des rues désertes et je voulus me dénuder comme elle," (Ibid, 329).
70 "J'étails élevé dans un vol d'anges qui n'avaient ni corps ni têtes [...] je devins malheureux et me sentis abandonné comme on l'est en présence de DIEU" (*Madame Edwarda*, 330).

character's inebriation and the extremity of his sensation:

> I was pulled out of my dazed confusion by an only too human voice. Madame Edwarda's thin voice, like her slender body was obscene: "I guess what you want is to see the old rag and ruin," she said. Hanging on to the tabletop with both hands, I twisted around toward her. She was seated, she held one leg stuck up in the air, to open her crack yet wider she used fingers to draw the folds of skin apart. And so Madame Edwarda's "old rag and ruin" loured at me, hairy and pink, just as full of life as some loathsome squid. "Why," I stammered in a subdued tone, "why are you doing that?" "You can see for yourself," she said, "I'm GOD." "I'm going crazy – " "Oh, no you don't, you've got to see, look…" (150)[71]

The protagonist can only respond to Edwarda's command by shaking and sinking to his knees, an image that blends oral sex with prayer, and which bathes him in sweat and a feeling as if the pair "were losing themselves in a wind-freighted night, on the edge of the ocean" (150)[72].

---

71   "De mon hébétude, une voix, trop humaine, me tira.La voix de Madame Edwarda, comme son corps gracile, était obscène : – Tu veux voir mes guenilles? disait - elle. Les deux mains agrippées a la table, je me tournai vers elle. Assise, elle maintenait haute une jambe écartée : pour mieux ouvrir la fente, elle achevait de tirer la peau des deux mains. Ainsi les "guenilles" d'Edwarda me regardaient, velues et roses, pleines de vie comme un pieuvre répugnante. Je balbutiai doucement : – Pourquoi fais-tu cela? – Tu vois, dit-elle, je suis DIEU… – Je suis fou… – Mais, non, tue dois regarder : regarde! (Ibid, 330 - 331).
72   "comme si Edwarda et moi nous étions perdus dans une nuit de vent devant la mer" (Ibid, 331).

Bataille's insistence on both the body at its most visceral and base – "rag and ruin," "loathsome," "sweating" – and the sublime, "wind" and "ocean," gives the account its paradoxical strength and suggestiveness, creating a sort of mystical unity between the basest elements of experience and their loftiest implications, affirming their difference to the point of negating it. And the protagonist's simultaneous confusion at and embrace of Edwarda's mad claims only highlights this; his response to Edwarda's affirmation of her godhood lends the deeply muddy scene its authority and interpellates the reader, generating the underlying meaning of everything that subsequently builds from this self-annihilating ecstasy at "The Mirrors." From here, the narrator and Madame Edwarda – who, by dressing in a mask and domino for the procession, transforms herself further, covering her face and thus obliterating her identity – will undertake a drunken, but strangely ceremonial, reeling through the streets of Paris. This culminates in an anonymous sexual encounter with a taxi driver. So formal is this movement from street to brothel to the Portes Saint-Denis and through the streets once more that Allan Stoekl has read it as ritualistic and noted parallels between the book's narrative unfolding and that of the Mass, suggesting that the substitution of the body of the prostitute for God may parallel the transformation of the base substance of the host into deity, and that the various transitions in the narrative reflect those of such ceremonies as the "Mass of the Catechumens" (83). The account of the nocturnal perambulation, however, is also punctuated with repetitive references to the night, the heavens, and their overwhelming presence. For example, we read as they exit the brothel: "Edwarda, something alien; above our heads, a starry sky, mad and void. I thought I was going to stagger and fall, but didn't" (*Madame Edwarda*,152)[73]. The trope arises again later: "Desperate I pointed to the empty sky curved above us" (154)[74]; and again: "not knowing why, its teeth chattering in the lashing wind: the immensity, the night engulfs it and, all on purpose, that living self is there just in order....'not to know' " (159)[75]. In the relatively short text of the novella such reiteration of a single image constitutes insistence. Time and again, Edwarda's body and the protagonist's desire are related to the void, the night, emptiness and the limits of both knowledge and experience in a kind of visionary transport that unites ontological extremes such as the genitals and the cosmos. This floods the protagonist and the sentences with a terrible sense of import that can only be partially contained by the words used to render them, creating an evasiveness or blank space reiterated in the several times the narrator seems to lose sight of Edwarda herself, who is simultaneously a synecdoche for the numinous universe that so overwhelms, and an echo of the two prostitutes who vanish at the book's opening. However, the disappearance of the women and the emphasis given to the infinite void of space are far from the most striking examples of blank space in *Madame Edwarda*. Bataille inserts several lines of ellipses into the narrative at the very moment the protagonist and Edward "go up" together (151), provocatively insisting on the limits of knowledge, the

73 "Edwarda, étrangère, un ciel étoilé, vide et fou, sur nos têtes : je pensais vaciller mais je marchais" (Ibid, 333).
74 "Désesperé, je lui montrai sur nous le ciel vide" (Ibid, 334).
75 "ne sachant pourquoi, de froid demeuré tremblant...; l'immensité, la nuit l'environnent et, tout exprès, il est là pour ... 'ne pas savoir' " (Ibid, 339).

breaking point of language even as he uses it – underlining the sheer impossibility of ever ultimately grasping everything and the sort of blind ecstasy, stammering or silent, that reaching such a breaking point calls up. The powerful presence of such unifying motifs is what ties this fiction to Bataille's theoretical and philosophical work on mysticism and highlights the extent to which, more broadly, his "erotic novels and stories should also be understood as explorations and representations of inner experience" (Poppenberg, 113).

Written on the eve of World War II, *Inner Experience* is the first volume of Bataille's *Summa Atheologica*, which also includes *Guilty* and *On Nietzsche*, and constitutes his most systematic attempt to articulate a theory of mystical experience. As the title of the three-volume work suggests, Bataille's theory is formulated at least partly in response to Aquinas and is atheistic in nature. However, the author specifically acknowledges that the work concerns, for lack of a better word, "spiritual" experience, despite this atheism: "[b]y inner experience I understand that which one usually calls mystical experience: the states of ecstasy, of rapture, at least of meditated emotion" (*Inner Experience*, 3)[76]. His sense of such experience, however, is not centred on theophany as is the case in much traditional mysticism, but rather on an experience of the extreme limit, beyond which lies no deity but rather silence, darkness and the void – "non-knowledge" – as he will repeatedly put it in this work, as he does here: "NON-KNOWLEDGE COMMUNICATES ECSTASY. Non-knowledge

[76] "J'entends par *expérience intérieure* ce que d'habitude on nomme *expérience mystique* : les états d'extase, de ravissement, au moins d'émotion méditée" (*L'expérience intérieure*, 15).

is ANGUISH before all else. In anguish, there appears a nudity which puts one into ecstasy" (52, upper case in original).[77] Thus, the experience is resolutely without the consolation of the divine and becomes a transport that unites ecstasy with a kind of agony because there is nothing beyond it but the void; "Bataille is in effect editing the dictionary, striking from the rubric 'mysticism' every allusion to God" (Connor, 57), and this abandonment stands as an acknowledgement that such experience always leaves us faced with a blankness, hence the stress given to "ANGUISH." Moreover, in light of Bataille's commitment to working in both philosophical and erotic forms, the presence of nudity in his description underlines something of the quality he ascribes to such "nonknowledge" in much the same way the incorporation of the ellipses does in *Madame Edwarda*.

This notion takes precise and poetic shape in part five of *Inner Experience*, titled "Manibus Date Lilia Plenis". In this section Bataille shifts from the prose in which the overwhelming majority of *Inner Experience* is composed to several pages of lineated verse. In these poetic fragments a deeply personal expression of the limit of experience is essayed and images appear that clearly echo some of the repeated motifs found in *Madame Edwarda*. He writes of the anguished transport that is his subject: "Who am I / not 'me' no no / but the desert the night the immensity / what I am / What are desert immensity

---

77 LE NON-SAVOIR COMMUNIQUE L'EXTASE. Le non-savoir est tout d'abord ANGOISSE. Dans l'angoisse apparaît la nudité, qui extasie" (Ibid, 66).

night animal/soon irrevocable Nothingness" (162)[78] and, on the next page, "Star/which I am/ O Death/thunderous star/mad bell of my death." (163)[79]. Here the "limit' implied in any "limit experience" is given form in images that define the extreme point of any number of possibilities: death, as the limit of biological life, desert as a similar image of barrenness or emptiness which is echoed in the invocation of "nothingness," and the immensity of sky and the stars which can only be read as metonym for the extreme edge of the physical universe. The transformation of "star" to "bell" further complicates this, blurring entire categories of being in their dissolution. In addition, as was discussed above, these are images that animate the most extreme moments of tension in *Madame Edwarda*: moments in which her body is described in terms of its fragility – her genitals as "rag and ruin" (a very free translation), or her face covered with a mask and hence obliterated in order to go into the world, and in which the stars themselves oppress the protagonist by their distance and remind him of his transitoriness and insignificance, plunging him into a transcendent anguish that corresponds precisely in every detail to the experience investigated by Bataille in his philosophical treatise.

Thus, inner experience is an experience at the extreme limits of what is possible (presaging another key Bataille title and theme, *L'impossible*.) Inner experience, Bataille argues, creates

78   "Qui suis-je/pas "moi" non non/mais le désert la nuit l'immensité/ qui je suis/qu'est-ce/désert immensité nuit bête/vite néant sans retour" (Ibid, np)

79   "Étoile/je la suis/ô mort/étoile de tonnerre/folle cloche de ma mort." (Ibid, np)

a rapture or ecstasy that is meaningful, but self-justifying, requiring no transcendent referent. It is a form of "forbidden" knowledge/non-knowledge and hence "occult" or "hidden." It, in a pointed variant on the crucial surrealist aim, "attains in the end the fusion of object and subject, being as subject non-knowledge, as object the unknown" (9)[80] which is to say an absolute that accommodates uncertainty, and thus requires no justification. This truth, a "nothingness" which cannot be expressed or contained, is for Bataille what remains after an innately human will to identify the self with the universe or a creator is exhausted. Among the modalities of this experience of the "extreme limit" Bataille outlines, aside from the sexual transgression already discussed, are a peculiarly ferocious sort of contemplation, laughter, and sacrifice and/or the communal experience of death. In every case, however, such ecstasy is marked by a "[f]orgetting of everything. Deep descent into the night of existence. Infinite ignorant pleading, to drown oneself in anguish. To slip over the abyss and in the completed darkness experience the horror of it" (36)[81]. Thus, inner experience, "at the extreme limit of the possible [...] requires a renouncement: to cease wanting to be everything" (22)[82]. And, although Bataille opposes this "inner experience" to what he calls "project" in the text, the purposeful approach to life/work which is an attempt to create a *telos*, or organizing principle for

80 "L'expérience atteint pour finir la fusion de l'objet et du sujet, étant comme sujet non-savoir, comme objet l'inconnu." (Ibid, 21)
81 "Oubli de tout. Profonde descente dans la nuit de l'existence. Supplication infinie de l'ignorance, se noyer d'angoisse. Se glisser au-dessus de l'abîme dans l'obscurité achevée en éprouver l'horreur," (Ibid, 49).
82 "à l'extrême du possible demande un renoncement néanmoins : cesser de vouloir être tout," (Ibid, 34).

mental life, he insists on its meaningfulness.

Bataille writes about this pre- or non-verbal ecstasy at length, an apparent paradox that is inherent in his conception of the experience itself. Indeed, he puts this paradox at the centre of it when he writes, "Principle of inner experience: to emerge through project from the realm of project" (46)[83] and, unlike many mystics, he further asserts "[it] is not beyond expression – one doesn't betray it if one speaks of it [...]" (3)[84]. So central is this assertion, in fact, that Connor claims "Bataille's deepest conviction is that language can and does communicate even the most interior of experience." (3). However, Bataille makes such experience inseparable from its expression in language because "just as 'profound communication demands silence', silence in turn demands communication" (Connor, 51). Thus, in this properly speaking occultural turn, as it is implicated in some form of the discursive at least, the relation of account and experience operates even at the place where both reach their limit.

CULTURES OF QUEER RITUAL

The gay liberation movement, too, begins with a recognition of the broad significance of erotic experience, and its implication in accounts of what was once seen as the outer limit of the possible – or at least the acceptable – as Gayle Rubin demonstrates in the "charmed circle" model outlined in "Thinking Sex" (151-

83   "Principe de l'expérience intérieure : sortir par un projet du domaine du projet" (*L'expérience intérieure*, 60).
84   "Elle n'est pas ineffable, on ne la trahit pas si l'on en parle..." (*L'expérience intérieure*, 15 - 16).

152). Specifically, Gay Lib articulates an oppositional position to current ideas of normalcy while insisting on the possibility of multiple accounts, of polyvocality. The early partisans of gay liberation were deeply concerned with countering established ideas about homosexuality and some were consequently willing to investigate a variety of more marginal conceptual structures about other aspects of reality, including those of the occult.

Of course, sexuality was a central component of many other historical systems of occult thought and practice as well, so it is unsurprising to find it a constitutive thread in radical queer discourses (as it is of Bataille's not-unrelated vision). Hugh Urban writes of this,

> Practitioners of sexual magic would also turn to explicitly non-productive and – by the standards of their surrounding society – morally deviant and socially transgressive acts such as homosexual intercourse, masturbation, sadomasochism, [....]as the most powerful means to unleash a supernatural source of power. And [...] it is no accident that the rise of sexual magic in the West went hand in hand with the new search for sexual freedom, feminism, and gay rights. (Urban, 4)

Urban's assertions find remarkable support, in fact, in much gay literature and film to emerge from the ferment of pre-liberation and early liberationist praxis. Two works, by Kenneth Anger and William Carney, are illustrative of some of the implications of this. Both date from the period immediately prior to the development of an organized gay movement, a period marked by the flowering of the '60s counterculture and the beginnings of the sexual revolution: a moment of intense cultural/political change, but also one in which traditional identities, sexual, racial and gender identities among them, were being transformed. It was also a time that saw the transition of gay life from a condition of nearly total social invisibility into one that, while still marginal, was at least somewhat on the public radar. These texts, therefore, provide insight into the psychosocial dynamics of the movement as it takes shape.

Kenneth Anger's now canonical 1963 short experimental film *Scorpio Rising* is a paradigmatic case of a work reflecting these tensions. Ostensibly the portrait of a group of young bikers,[85] it becomes in Anger's hands a far more complex and polyphonous work that brings the homoeroticism bubbling under the surface of 1960s motorcycle culture to the surface and layers atop it a whole range of occult symbolism, while posing vital questions about community building and self-fashioning. The film announces its interests from the first frames, even before the title appears. It opens with the logo of Anger's production company, named for Shakespeare's mischievous fairy Puck and bearing his signature tagline "What fools these mortals be..." immediately pointing to the film's self-referential

85   The choice of bikers as a subject is of significance here too. Motorcycle gangs were a broad cultural presence in the early and mid 60s: note, for example Hunter S. Thompson's landmark book, *Hell's Angels* (1966) and the proliferation of "biker films" as a genre, including, among others *The Leather Boys* (1964), *Outlaw Motorcycles* (1966), *The Wild Angels* (1966). Nor should one neglect an earlier work, *The Wild One* (1953) which has found a place in the Hollywood canon. In the context of this discussion it is also significant that bikers occupy an "outlaw" status analogous in some ways to that of gay people at this period.

aestheticism and – given the supernatural, or fictional, status of fairies as well as their association with homosexuality (a thread clearly picked up by the Radical Faeries in the 1970s) – its concern with different orders of being. This is followed by a young man carefully polishing the chrome of his motorcycle, a clear indication of the film's obsessive interest in surfaces/appearances and their meanings, a connection highlighted by an image of boots spliced into the sequence evoking the worlds of fashion and fetishism at one fell swoop. It is only after this that the film's title appears, as a series of chrome studs applied to the title character's black leather jacket just before he turns to expose his torso, bare under the garment, which the camera lovingly frames at belt-line in order to highlight the homoerotic content. The muscular young man is juxtaposed with an image of a scorpion in bright red. Within these few minutes Anger succeeds in foreshadowing the film's concerns and trajectory with astounding economy.

The image of the scorpion merits more consideration as it recurs throughout the film. An obvious reference to the title, the scorpion is the emblem of the astrological sign "Scorpio," traditionally associated with sexuality, the occult, death and some forms of violence. The figure's redness is also of note as it is an unusual colour for a scorpion in the natural world but is traditionally associated with the planet Mars, thought, before the discovery of Pluto[86], to rule the sign Scorpio. This emblem points to Anger's concern with occult colour symbolism which, although more prominent in films like *Inauguration of the*

86   A comprehensive source of information concerning such magical "correspondences" is: Stephen Skinner, Ph.D. *The Complete Magician's Tables.* Woodbury: Llewellyn Publications. 2007..

Pleasure Dome and *Invocation of My Demon Brother* (discussed by Noble in her article "The Light Behind the Lens") is clearly present in this work too.

From this powerfully signifying opening, the film follows the biker gang as they prepare for a party. The preparation includes the polishing and customizing of their motorcycles and the selection and donning of some highly ornamented garments and accessories, all accompanied by self-examination in mirrors with great attention (conventionally "feminine" behaviour despite the men's carefully articulated butchness) to the details of the outfit. Further highlighting the sexual suggestiveness of the sequence is a moment in which one man (bare-chested under his jacket once again) stands, legs spread, over a traffic cone. The cone, and the legs of his jeans, whose inseams are trimmed in fabric of contrasting colour, form a powerful inverted "v" shape pointing towards his genitals. Here the traditional association of homosexuality and concern with appearances is given an unsubtle evocation, heightened by Bobby Vinton crooning "she wore blue velvet" on the soundtrack in a way that can only be heard as camp. Moreover, this sartorial preparation takes place in spaces that are, to say the least, highly-charged semiotically. In one instance, the room's walls are covered in clippings and photos: movie star portraits, caricatures, badges and a patch bearing yet another image of Scorpio/the scorpion. (Figure 5 and Figure 6). The man lounges while *The Wild One* plays on a small TV set in his room, and he reads comics. The presence of so many self-conscious signifiers clearly requests that the viewer read this scene, that he apply a hermeneutically engaged eye to all of

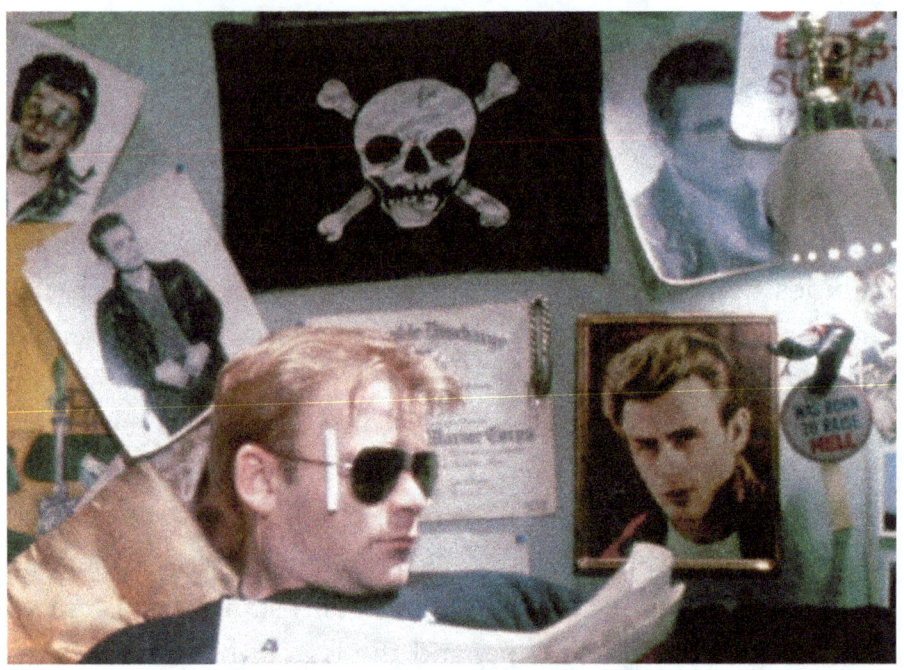

Figure 5. Still image from *Scorpio Rising*, Kenneth Anger, 1963.

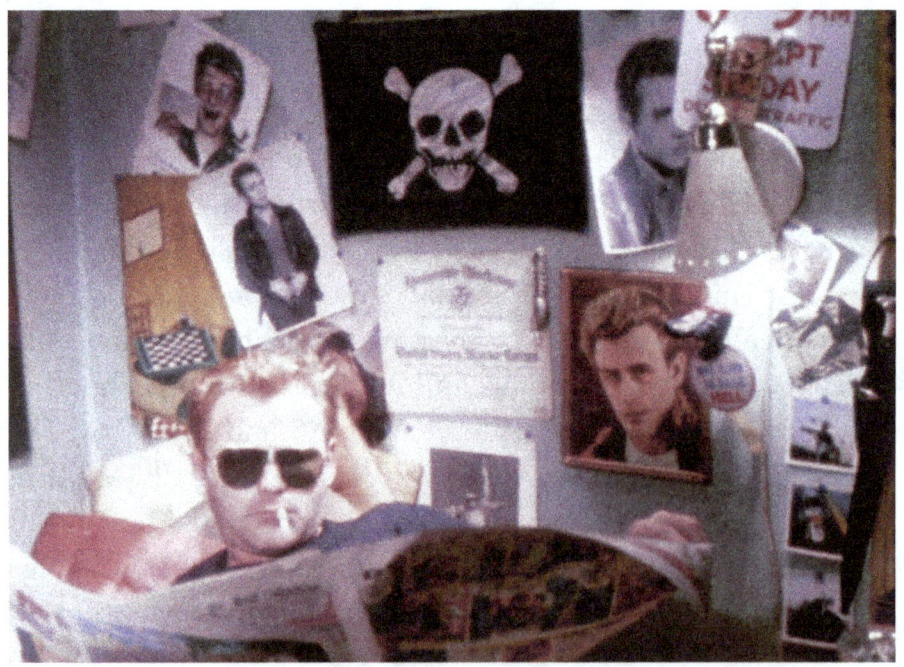

Figure 6. Still image from *Scorpio Rising*, Kenneth Anger, 1963.

its details. And the room is a whirlpool of suggestion: a young biker watches a film about young bikers as he prepares to meet his crew of young bikers highlighting the extent to which his identity is a product of his own spectatorship. In the comics he is reading allusions to the homoerotic abound (one panel shows a man asking another if he is offering to "share his room" while another shows two boys saying that the differences between them are small and consist of one being "dirtier.") In this confluence of preparing the body, erotic self-evaluation, and a focus on the Barthesean scriptibility of the social (and intimate) environment one cannot avoid the suggestion of creative work and of transformation on the psychic and physical level.

This moment of the encounter with the self, however domestic, is overlaid with the presence of magick (the spelling favoured by Aleister Crowley) in the form of repeated images of skulls, a Scorpio patch and a badge on the wall stating the occupant was "born to raise hell:" a simple colloquialism but one that still carries a whiff of the Witches' Sabbat. When one adds to this edifice of codes the pop tunes accompanying the images, the hermeneutic bacchanal reaches the bursting point; "Devil in Disguise" by Elvis Presley succeeds in troubling any simple reading of this scene through both its inversion of gender and its invocation of the dark arts. Not yet halfway through its runtime *Scorpio Rising* has erected a profoundly generative network of occultural significations in which a secretive male society is established as self-conscious, fraught with buried erotic tensions and concerned with the diabolical.

All of this escalates in the film's second half where we see the club come together: they arrive at what one presumes is their clubhouse in a kind of costumed procession – in which the disguises donned include skeletons, demons, and wand-like batons. This procession, and the later horseplay, laden with implied BDSM activities, is given further interpretive complexity by its being broken up with footage from an obscure film about the life of Christ – adding more ritualistic suggestiveness – and the fact that the Everly Brothers' hit song "Torture" plays on the soundtrack.

One must recognize in these esoteric allusions Anger's self-declared artistic (and magickal) project. In his notes to a 1966 screening of the *Magick Lantern Cycle* cited by Powell (53), Anger writes that his "Lifework" is Magick and his Magical Weapon the "Cinematograph," indicating the connection he conceives of between film and sorcerous conjuration and highlighting the centrality of such symbolism for any exegesis of his work. In *Scorpio Rising*, his endeavour to make of his films a kind of "spell" climbs to its highest point in the motorcycle race at its climax. Leading up to it, the titular character presides, masked, over a darkened altar in a ceremony that appears to be both a kind of church desecration/black mass and an exhortation to the gang members (Figure 7) as they begin the race that ultimately leads to the death of one of their numbers in what can, at Anger's own suggestion, be read as a sacrificial rite for the transformation of American culture (74), thus connecting it to a larger social project. The young rider's death is further linked to magical symbolism by the return of the scorpion logo from the film's opening, this time in a sinister inverted position suggesting malevolent magic, and the bathing of the deceased in a red wash of light by the dome lights on the police

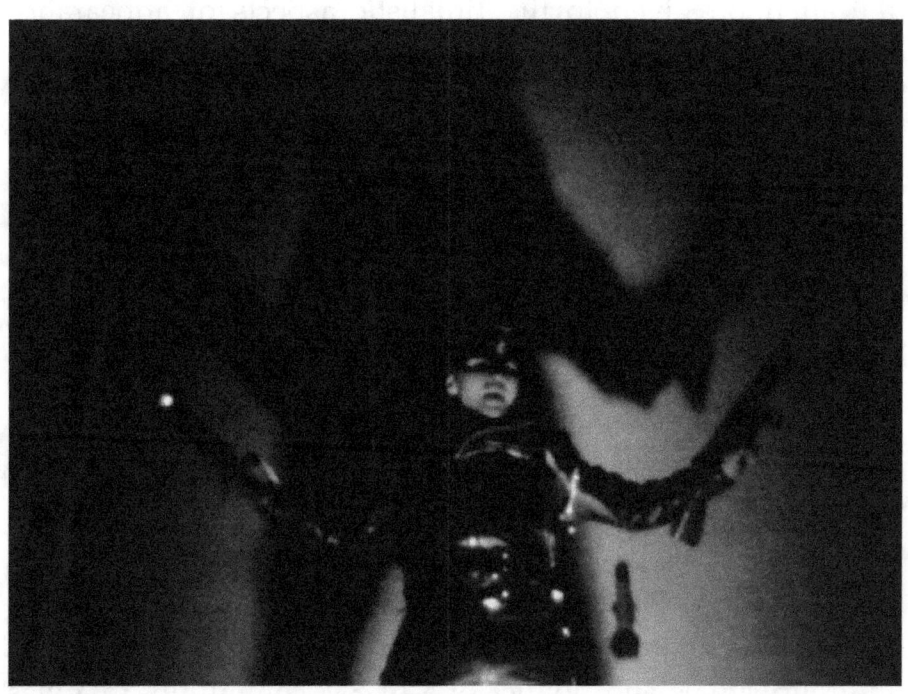

Figure 7. Still image from *Scorpio Rising*, Kenneth Anger, 1963

car's roof. Read this way, the film's progress from the young men's "vesting" themselves, assembling in a formal procession (similar in some ways to that found in Bataille's novella by Stoekl) through to a sacrificial incident, structures the film in two pertinent ways: first, as a cinematic magical rite in keeping with Anger's declared interests and second, through the attention given to the ritualistic aspects of appearance and gesture, as a statement regarding ritual magic as spiritual practice and a form of self-fashioning.

Moreover, *Scorpio Rising* is not the only ritualized and eroticized work concerned with queer self-fashioning. A ritual or spiritual dimension to the homoerotic self-fashioning of bikers and their kin – leathermen – is explored in another immediately "pre-Stonewall" text as well: William Carney's *The Real Thing*. First published in 1968, a mere year before the Stonewall Riots, Carney's book is a unique document of the first generation of a gay male leather subculture. The novel is a one-sided epistolary narrative in which an older man corresponds with his nephew, just coming-out as gay and a BDSM practitioner. In the sequence of letters the nephew is given a "sentimental," and erotic, education regarding the protocols, in-group rituals and politics of a BDSM community that was deeply underground at the time of novel's publication. At this juncture, it is of interest to point out, given the constitution of the novel as "letters," that in his work on ascesis, Foucault also notes the tremendous significance of letters in such practices during the Classical period (*Technologies*, 27).

Pointedly, *The Real Thing*'s letters consistently describe sadomasochistic practice in very precise, indeed ceremonial, terms and characterize it as the "work" and more tellingly, as "the way" or "path" with all the inherent spiritual connotations that necessarily cling to such descriptors. These implications are highlighted by a formality of tone and given particular relevance in a letter in which the narrator classifies the various types of BDSM players. He identifies established players as " Purists," "Exemplars," and "the Perfect" (Carney, 18), with these designations being based on the characteristics and skills the individuals have developed in the "work." The "ranks" are specific and evocative; the "Purists," for example, are also sometimes referred to as "oblates," a term whose most common use characterizes persons who have affiliated themselves to a monastic order without taking vows. The term "Perfect" echoes the title members of the heretical medieval sect of Cathars gave to their religious leaders – the "Perfect" (*Perfecti*) – because they were thought to have achieved a spiritual condition beyond sin.[87] In passages like these Carney points to the ways gay leathermen are not merely a very secretive community, but a kind of secret society concerned with deliberate, significant ritual, and spiritual work. Returning to these statuses later in the novel, he writes,

> For the ranks of Exemplar and the Perfect are equally efficacious and so equally honourable. They may be likened to the secular and the regular clergy. Their great difference is in intensity. If Exemplars are admired and respected, the Perfect are venerated and feared. The

87   For a popular discussion of Catharism and its history see: Stephen O'Shea. *The Perfect Heresy: The Life and Death of the Cathars*. London: Profile Books. 2001.

exemplary ritual is like a dance. It is, in fact, several highly stylized and erotic dances, beginning with the encounter, the look, and ending in contemplation. The perfected rite, on the other hand, is something quite different: silent, motionless, manipulatory – the *manus gloriae*. (42)

In this passage the theme is inscribed in the very lexis: "venerated," "ritual," "rite," and "contemplation" all evoke spiritual practice. The sudden appearance of the words "manus gloriae" raise the implications to another level. The hand of glory is an artefact of medieval magic: the preserved left hand of a hanged person used in diabolical sorcery.[88]

A shared setting of all-male, leather-clad communities, clearly unites *Scorpio Rising* and *The Real Thing*, and while the discretion and secrecy, even ambiguity, that seem to surround the milieux of these works may be partly attributable to their creation prior to the emergence of the gay liberation movement, the texts clearly point to deeper reasons for such secrecy: namely that these activities are spiritual practices, "mysteries" in the sense of those celebrated at Eleusis. Both also end on a troubling kind of sacrifice: the young biker dying in an accident and the narrator of the novel ruined in a perverse and cruel erotic game. Such a reading takes into account the many and complex signifiers pointing to the ways in which the inhabitants of these worlds are involved in a kind of spiritual or magical

88   The construction and use of the macabre object are detailed in the grimoire *Le Petit Albert*, a number of commercial editions of which are available. The information may also be found in the Grimoire Encyclopedia online here: https://www.grimoire.org/grimoire/petit-albert/

praxis, a path of self-development or *ascesis*, and one that – as is suggested by the self-conscious display of such praxis in these works – is not simply a question of representation, but one built into the texts' forms and language by their creators and troubling their surface. Recognition of this praxis is necessary for their occultural interpretation by readers/viewers, and this consequently in some ways unites them in community too via this very system of shared language, symbols and initiatory ritual.

Moreover, there were also men profoundly interested in witchcraft and the occult among the founders of the very first post-Stonewall gay activist organizations like the Gay Liberation Front (GLF) and the Gay Activists Alliance (GAA) including, notably, Leo Martello and Arthur Evans.

PHANTASMATIC FAERIE

Arthur Evans was a prominent figure in the early gay liberation movement, active, like Martello, in both the GLF and the GAA; Evans, in fact, was one of the founders of the latter organization (Lauritsen 29). Evans' broadest influence may, however, lie in his publication of the study *Witchcraft and the Gay Counterculture* (1978) in which he argues for a deep connection between homoerotically inclined men, pagan religions, and witchcraft. He draws the line linking magic and the most radical positions of gay liberation explicitly, writing, "I believe that we must bring about a massive withdrawal of allegiance from the dominant institutions of industrialism [...] And we must demystify ourselves to overcome the belief instilled in us that we can't heal ourselves, educate ourselves, create our own religion, or wage warfare on our own behalf. We can do all these things – and more!" (146) and "[i]f we are to to overthrow the industrial patriarchy, I believe we must tap into deeper energies, energies that the ruling classes of Christianity and industrialism have always desperately tried to deny and repress. These are the energies of magic" (148). *Witchcraft and the Gay Counterculture* makes a consistent occultural case for the usefulness of magic and ritual as epistemological and political tools, as ways of experiencing and occupying the world with applications in daily life and the networks of the social. Evans had been interested in such possibilities prior to publishing the book; he "founded [a] fairy circle in the mid-1970s" (Conner, 269) to discuss and explore such ideas, and it was most likely those real time explorations that led to the book and his declaration in it that "[w]e look forward to regaining our ancient historical roles as medicine people, healers, prophets, shamans, and sorcerers" (*Counterculture*, 154-155).

Evans followed up this volume with two more groundbreaking books. In 1984 he staged a production of his new translation of Euripides' *The Bacchae, one* that heightened its ritualistic elements, at the Valencia Rose Cabaret in San Francisco; the translation would be published by St. Martin's Press, with critical and historical commentary by Evans, in 1988 as *The God of Ecstasy: Sex-Roles and the Madness of Dionysos.* Evans, in these works, presents a feminist/gay liberationist reading of the myth of Dionysus in which the god is positioned in opposition to patriarchal values such as the repression of both feeling and sensuality, and militarism. The author would also compose an explicit analysis of patriarchal thought (published in 1997), the *Critique of Patriarchal Reason,* his most systematic philosophical work. Evans' thorough and sustained investigation of the ancient world, the Dionysian impulse, and ritual has led one critic to sum up his somewhat underground significance thus: "Evans is the nearest thing to a gay Nietzsche, a prophet, philosopher and artist in one" (McLeary, 130).

Of course, McLeary's reading of the work's details is not uniformly so hagiographic, nor is that of some other recent scholarship, that of Conner for example. Exception has been taken to aspects of Evans' research and certain claims in *Counterculture,* but such over-reaches are less pertinent to our analysis here than the undeniable influence Evans' ideas have had on gay politics and culture since the 1970s; his ideas about queer men and spiritual life have been an important thread in an ongoing subcultural tradition. Evans' writing and organizing of the Faerie Circle in the 70s, along with the work of Harry Hay during the same period, constitutes the founding matrix out of which the Radical Faeries' "movement" emerges at the "Spiritual Conference for Radical Fairies" held at a desert sanctuary near Tucson in 1979 (Adler, 341).

The Faeries are a loosely organized group of — largely — gay (and bisexual) men who hold that there is something psychologically and spiritually specific to gay, or homoerotically–inclined, men and that many cultures have historically recognized and honoured this. In response to this insight, they are consciously creating (or attempting to recreate) a spiritual and ritual tradition attuned to that specificity or role, and the social, emotional, and spiritual needs of the homoerotically-inclined that draws from the neo-pagan and goddess-spirituality movements (Adler), the spiritual traditions of pre-technological cultures, and gay traditions of gender play and camp. These emergent spiritual practices can be viewed productively as a form of cultural and religious bricolage in the sense articulated by Savastano: "the various ways that individuals and communities of gay men spiritologize [sic] at the grassroots level, spinning, weaving, and otherwise, synthesizing their religious visions and practices, thereby employing diverse spiritual idioms" from both existing traditions and "their firsthand experiences as liminal and stigmatized persons" (15). Furthermore, the informality implied in the characterization "bricolage" is reflected in the extremely loose organization that characterizes Faeries as well, making it, in some ways, "almost easier today to say what RFs [Radical Faeries] are not and don't believe than what they are and do believe" (McCleary, 147).

Such complexity and amorphousness aside, however, it remains possible to identify several shared core beliefs. An early declaration by Harry Hay unambiguously frames the Faeries' occultural project as having political, spiritual, and most importantly creative, aspects:

Fairies must begin creating their new world through fashioning for themselves supportive Families of Conscious Choice within which they can explore, in loving security of shared consensus, the endless depths and diversities of the new revealed subject-SUBJECT inheritances of the Gay Vision! Let us gather therefore

[162]

– in secure and consecrated places... To re-invoke from ancient ashes our Fairy Circle... To dance... To meditate – not in the singular isolation of Hetero subject-OBJECT praxis, but rather in Fairy Circles reaching out to one another in subject–SUBJECT evocation... To find new ways to cherish one another... To invent new rhyme and reason and ritual replacing those obliterated in the nightmare of our Oppression – *and so*, in fact, *re-invent* ourselves....(263)

Hay's insistence on an essentialist "subject-SUBJECT" consciousness is one of the key epistemological underpinnings of Faerie theory and praxis, "based on the notion that gay people experience and relate to the world in a fundamentally unique way [...] a way which is integral to the well-being of themselves as individuals, and that of the world as a whole" (Rodgers, 35). Thus, although such an essentialist claim is subject to the same critiques *any* essentialist claim is, the notion gives rise to an embodied Faerie praxis that has value beyond the merely theoretical for participants: it is a practice giving rise to particular kinds of experience. Faeries seek to cultivate such consciousness through Faerie rituals that are collectively developed in a trial and error process with broad implications. Furthermore, like surrealists, Faeries understand eros as central to their vision quest:

[sex] itself is often the source for gay men's religious visioning [...] [i]t is their outsider or liminal status that makes it possible [...and...] though not always the case,

sex is often a means by which gay men enter heightened states of consciousness (some would say states of ecstasy) (Savastano, 13)

The confluence of homosexual desire with ritual, affect ,and altered consciousness in faerie magic is also consciously operative in the work of contemporary American poet CA Conrad. In an online interview the poet acknowledges that "for many years [he's] been steeped in the occult" and has a history of "going to witch camps and pagan gatherings" (Beckett), and that involvement with the occult world has had impact on his poetic practice. Indeed his recent collections, such as *Ecodeviance: (Soma)tics for a Future Wilderness* and *While Standing in Line for Death,* are centred around "a practice of bodily ritual, a practice the unfolds on his blog as well as in the pages of his poetry collections" (Herd). The very name Conrad gives to these ritual practices, "(Soma)tics," points to their content and intended function. It implies both somatic as, of, or concerned with, the body and "soma" the ritual intoxicant associated with immortality and the divine in the Vedic tradition.[89] In these rituals Conrad undertakes a series of specific, embodied actions, often public ones, that "[demand] his absolute attention. [and] [a]fterward, having situated himself in the 'extreme present,' he [takes] extensive notes. [which provide] the basis for new poems." Furthermore, these rituals are "not just processes – they are part of the poems themselves" (Ridker). The continuity of the ritual practice and the poetry is, moreover, visible in its publication; in the books the ritual instructions

89   See https://en.wikipedia.org/wiki/Soma_(drink)

appear alongside the completed verse, a sort of invitation to the reader to replicate the experience (or experiment) for him or herself. To this extent they constitute a sort of grimoire, or wizard's handbook, but – as importantly – they recall surrealist experimentation with both trance states and automatic writing as compositional techniques even as they center *aesthesis* and other embodied forms of awareness; they "remind us that emotion is bodily, cognitive, and a meeting point between the world and ourselves" (Herd). The nexus vibrating between Conrad's work and these classic surrealist concerns, including trance and ritual, is further highlighted in his discussion of the work he's undertaken with dreams and in which he alters a therapeutic technique in order to make dreams appear in memory "in full colour and at lightning speed" (Beckett). This is a practice with clear parallels to the surrealists' publication of dream records and other oneiric texts so rigorously analyzed by Breton in *The Communicating Vessels*.

Eileen Myles, however, points to other elements of this nexus in her analysis of the opening poem of *The Book of Frank*. In her reading of the text she points to the profound concern with eros and embodiment animating Conrad's poetry, which is shared with generations of surrealist and queer poets, specifically in these lines:

Why doesn't my son have a cunt?
what has happened?
what a WICKED world!
DARK!
and spinning

on its one

good leg!

In her reading Myles points to the text's debt to surrealism in the way in which it "[implies] among other things the dissociative and destabilizing states of sex. Like what is this thing I'm sucking on. Surrealism was part, I think of a pattern of wildness [...]" (153). Myles choice of the word "wildness" is significant here. It is in this bringing together of body, magic, and poetry in the service of wildness – which is to say, freedom – that makes Conrad so interesting a figure in the confluence of poetics and praxis that may mark the space of a Queer Surrealism, the way in which he points to one possible emergence of it as a horizon towards which one might work. Because in the end, it is this focus on functionality, this dedication to use-value bent to the transformation of both the self and the social that characterize both surrealism's, and gay liberation's, use of the tools of the esoteric, as it does their understanding of eros and their cultivation of aesthesis. Occulture too becomes a bridge to the unattainable utopian horizon. And one that can be reinvented time and again as the shining city appears on the horizon and slips below it once more.

CHAPTER 5
CONCLUSION

This book has its roots in an intuition regarding a kind of resonance operating between surrealism and gay liberation. Surrealism gave the world a new word and concept, that of the "surreal." The coinage rapidly found a place in the culture, but has, sadly, been détourned, diluted, and much misused in popular parlance over the years – a misuse decried by actual surrealists.[90] Gay liberation, for its part, has also transformed much of contemporary culture and added to the lexis to the extent that the word "gay" is now all but unusable to denote anything but same sex desire. From this initial intuition a number of questions naturally arose. In addressing those questions (such as: what can we learn by studying queer theories and practices alongside the ideas and practices of surrealism, or, what aesthetic and political concerns and techniques are common to both surrealism and queer writing and culture) significant overlaps in political and philosophical concerns, theory, and praxis emerged and made visible previously obscure connections between gay liberation / queer theory and

90   For a sense of some of the important objections raised by surrealists to such popular misuse see Ron Sakolsky's "Hands Off the Word Surreal! Manifesto" found in his book Surrealism and the Anarchist Imagination, (Eberhardt Press, 2023).

surrealism.

The investigation rapidly uncovered that foundational among these shared concerns is the notion of a horizon or ideality against which the world is not only experienced, but against which it is measured. Moreover both these intellectual/ creative traditions acknowledge that the horizon, towards which all of their activity is directed has never actually *been known*, nor do they necessarily hold any expectation that one might ever know it, and it is in that fact – at least partly – that such a horizon's value lies. Thus, the horizon allows for, indeed requires, perennial reconsideration, perennial hope, and perennially new pleasures in such hope and reflection. Both Muñoz and Breton posit an ideality whose agency arises from a simultaneous presence and absence, a co-constituting desirability and impossibility and one that arguably takes shape in similar, even parallel ways in both theoretical narratives.

Given that these conceptions of an ideality are rooted in their unachievability, their value lies in being an object of pursuit, which is to say they are implicated in *practice* in the *doing of things*. So, in addition to the foundational *(a)telos* with which we began, our analysis of the *corpora* of works generated by surrealism and gay liberation (and its inheritors) has shown three particular and recurrent forms such pursuit/praxis has taken: a centering of, and conscious investment in, the erotic, the cultivation of aesthesis, and, consequently, with it the attendant valorization of feeling and the senses, and, finally, an investment in and experimentation with forms and practices drawn from the esoteric tradition. This trio is neither coincidental nor haphazard; it points towards the very deliberate approach both intellectual tendencies took towards their activities, and the extent to which such work was conceived of as simultaneously both personal and political; these three areas, after all, offer the movements an ontology, an epistemology and a functioning set of heuristics or tools for judgement and problem solving.

Eros serves as a driving force for both movements; it is, as has been demonstrated, a source of psychic energy and a matrix of relationality underpinning approaches to life and the world both and one that, in the words of Breton *"rises above national differences and social hierarchies*, and [...] [is] a fundamental principle for moral as well as cultural progress [...] as well as a permanent force of anticipation" (*Mad Love*, 77, italics in the original).[91] Breton's sentiment is clearly echoed by some of the earlier manifestoes of the gay liberation movement and remain present in later queer writing through to the present day. Eros – desire or passionate love – has a significance for the movements far beyond that commonly accorded to it. An investment in aesthesis grows organically out of such an expansive conception of the erotic; a conception of the world as rooted in desire both requires and is complemented or completed by an epistemology – a model of knowledge – rooted in sensation and affect as necessary counterbalances to reason. If one's first prompting toward some other is rooted in eros, the response to it can only be affective and driven by sensation. It is an epistemology that is necessarily relational, concerned with how we touch, embrace, connect with what is

91   "*s'élève au-dessus des differences nationales et des hiérarchies sociales, et* [...] [est un] principe fondamental au progrès moral aussi bien que culturel [...] aussi bien qu'un comme force permanente d'anticipation," (*L'Amour fou*, 112-113).

outside of us, which is necessarily mediated by what is inside of us. The complexity of this is acknowledged in recent work by queer theorists like Tim Dean who writes: "I'm interested in how sex raises ethical questions insofar as it is understood as a privileged domain in which we encounter otherness. It is because erotic relations condense our ambivalence about alterity, not because one way of fucking is better than any other, that sex becomes a matter of ethical concern" (*Unlimited*, 180). In the cases of surrealism and gay liberation and its later queer inheritors, such an epistemology is an outgrowth of the deep investment in alternate forms of understanding relationality: specifically the connection of the self to a variety of *others* (human and non-human). These movements see that connection as foundational and – at least as importantly – as operating across a wide range of psychic registers. Furthermore, their understanding of that complexity leads to a conviction that such relationality is inadequately served by models of the social rooted in and evaluated by merely productive metrics, by the crudely instrumental. We see this in Breton's visions and Berlin's pornography with equal force.This acute awareness therefore drives queer and surrealist methods of interacting with the world, with *otherness,* that are beyond the traditions of rationalism or utlitarianism, ways such as the occult and the hermetic tradition. Such models of relationality, moreover, have the additional benefit of providing a methodology that steps outside the narrow rationalism of a post-Cartesian modernity which, as Bauduin suggests, "was considered restrictive and bourgeois" (10): a matter of some import for groups and individuals with explicitly revolutionary programmes, such as those that have been our subject here.

While the overlaps I identify between surrealism and gay liberation are determinant and generative, their main interest for this project has been how they open up possibilities for some synthesis of their social and political visions and creative methodologies. The object of this study has been the manner in which these two movements may, together, be understood to generate the possibilities of a Queer Surrealism distinct from, though in relation to, its progenitors and whose potential emerges from reading these ideas and techniques against each other and through the forms in which they are embedded. Therefore, it is from these sources that my project points to a conception of Queer Surrealism as a deliberate, and/or self-conscious, creative deployment of desire (an unconscious drive) through practices that work to shut down the either/or logics of normative views of the self as always distinct from *otherness* and from communities construed as pre-existing social formations into which one situates oneself. I see Queer Surrealism as a conception of subjectivity as structured and defined by relationship – that is to say, by its *contact with* otherness, whether such otherness takes the shape of the unconscious, the world, or other people (among many more possibilities). Moreover, even as Queer Surrealism is construed, or constructed, as conceiving of – in an echo of Masson's "collective experience of individualism" cited above – subjectivity as *defined by* relationality, it sees relationality itself as a praxis, a something one does; one cultivates relationship (in senses both quasi-agricultural, one grows them, and aesthetic, one designs or refines them) and so it takes subjectivity too as a praxis. Although the subject is formed by forces always outside one, it is possible to *work (or play) with* such forces.

Thus it will be useful in drawing conclusions regarding this Queer Surrealism to assess a number of its specific manifestations in turn: the ways in which such praxis takes particular shape, first as a body of texts, notions and knowledge, then as a model of subjectivity, and finally, its social contours, the way it takes form as community.

In some ways, making meaning from some experience or text is always provisional at the deepest psychic level: the process of thinking through, of inscription and reinscription is a necessary component of such signifying, and the entry of texts and meanings into the hands and minds of readers is perpetually renewed and renewable precisely because it is rooted in *ongoing practice*. Indeed what marks these works – novels, memoirs, films and poems – is the manner in which they not only accept their scriptibility, their reading and rereading, their constant repositioning and inevitable failure to close down, but self-consciously embrace it, even foreground it. These works are generative not because they enable smooth access to their meanings but because they work against that sort of transparency. The complexity of these texts creates a parallel complexity in their reception which in turn feeds back into a dizzying array of further contingent narratives within a space of spectatorship. They move towards a form of knowledge by engaging their viewers in a work of *poiesis*, which is to say of making more than interpreting, by engaging them in an act of readership/viewership that is self-conscious. Such readerly implication in the production of meanings is, one might argue, also the point of the insistence we have noted regarding a number of shared and repeated tropes and techniques.

MAKING: CONSCIOUSNESS COMMUNITY

Arising from this activated body of text and thought, a focus on desire and scriptibility as forms of relationality is especially pertinent for a Queer Surrealism because the constitution of a gay subject is never a given; the culture is not articulated to form queer subjects. Thus the question of how queer men form themselves into recognizable subjects and form a world able to accommodate such subjects takes on real urgency. Certainly, queer children very rarely grow up in queer families. Gay people, as Foucault and many other theorists have demonstrated are objects of knowledge and power and, until recently, very rarely the subjects of them. Gay people are always faced with taking their own becoming, individually and collectively in hand and one of the ways in which to do this is through representation. Brett Farmer writes of the specificity of acts of film spectatorship for many gay men that,

[Film] is a vital but exceedingly complex site for the production and performance of gay male identifications. It has assumed a vast range of productive functions and effects for gay subjectivities/cultures, enabling articulations of gay subcultural identity, fostering formations of gay desire and providing an endless source of material for the production of gay meanings.

[173]

(67)

Farmer's claim holds true for many non-filmic texts as well; his model allows us to read the complexity and frequent self-consciousness of the works examined here differently, and to see in them the mobilization of a particular awareness fostered by the queer experience of the closet and coming out (among others): the sense that the world isn't "made for me," that one doesn't easily fit into the world as it constructed; thus one is faced with having to remake oneself, or it, for life to become meaningful. And that if so much is true for oneself, it is surely true for others doing the same: one feels the proliferation of possible worlds – mobile ones that one has to pursue even as they slip away.

Which brings us to the place and function of such viewing, and such meanings, in this world. As gay liberation has forced open the closet to some extent, it has, as some of these texts testify, seen a proliferation of dissident or divergent gay subjectivities. That said, the "official" face of gay men in the media and the political world of electoral parties and governments seems, in recent years, to have grown, contrarily, increasingly homogeneous, largely focussed on marriage and other forms of assiimilation, and a problematic notion that "really, we're all the same." Whatever the positive outcomes of such a politics, and they are not negligible, there can be little doubt that it reduces difference; it restrains possible discourse and forecloses on many emerging subjectivities even as they take shape. Eve Sedgwick points to the significance of this in her aptly titled "Queer and Now" when she writes:" What if [...] there were a practice of valuing the ways in which meanings and institutions can be at loose ends with each other? What if the richest junctures [aren't] the ones where *everything means the same thing?*" (*Tendencies*, 6; Sedgwick's emphasis). That is why texts (novels, films, photographs) of the sort discussed here matter, why they are more than simply cultural artefacts or representations. If gay subjectivity does, at least partly, comprise an understanding of life, the world, and reality as multiple, and desire as the force that binds these things together and permits movement across them, then such texts are important. They become occasions of what Sedgwick calls in another essay "reparative reading;" the practices of reading and writing discussed here self-consciously embrace the overlapping of the real world and the utopian horizon as "additive and accretive" and "[want] to assemble and confer plenitude on an object that will then have resources to offer to an inchoate self" (*Touching Feeling*, 149). In doing this they affirm the world's elasticity, its relationship – and responsiveness – to desire and to imagination, and this in itself it the best answer to the "paranoid" stance and its suspicion of reparative motives as "aesthetic" or concerned with pleasure, and "reformist" or ameliorative (144). They move past the merely ameliorative by insisting on the importance of *making* and shared wonder as fundamental aims of any meaningful life or community. Insisting that, in fact, they are not trivial things but significant standards against which to test ideas, actions, forms, and arrangements of life and power. A more utopian idea would be hard to imagine.

The discussion of reading practices returns us to the idea of relationality itself as a praxis, which is central to any possible emergence of a Queer Surrealism because it cannot cohere in a simple confluence of interests or a common set of symbolic languages; these overlaps must come together in a sort of shared generative matrix in which interest, language, and action meet and co-create. Indeed, as I have stressed throughout this work what unites many of the interventions discussed in my postulation of a Queer Surrealism is the notion of practice. Whether it is a matter of occult practice, sexual practice, automatism, or shared, communitarian life, one of the crucial threads tying together the protean corpora examined in this work is that which suggests that the widest potentiality of life is predicated more on *deliberate action t*han pre-existing conditions. Practice is central because both surrealism and early queer radicalism articulate identities and communities predicated not on circumstances of birth (biological determinism gains greater presence in the discourse of gay politics later), or on simple assertion (despite the importance of the coming out process and its complexities), but on practices elaborated in the pursuit of shared goals. Thus Queer Surrealism manages to sidestep, in at least some ways, many of the theoretical pitfalls of identity claims whose essentialism so-often also requires the positing of a binary against which their specificity is made visible. Practice, after all, needs no validation beyond the doing, and in making this claim I embrace the sense of the word as denoting "any operation that provides or improves the actor's qualification for the next performance of the same operation"(Sloterdijk 5) whose resonance with the perpetually renewed pursuit of a utopian horizon is undeniable. The range of practices whose

overlap spans both of the groups at issue is significant, and has
already been approached in the critical literature: things like
the conscious cultivation of the erotic sense (Mahon, Székely);
the formation of small, closely-knit communities (Caws); the
interrogation and deliberate shaping of subjectivity (Foucault,
Butler, Dean); the practice of "openness" alluded to above,
whether it appears in the form of automatism (which Paz
has suggested is a form of meditation [49]) or cruising and
other forms of spontaneous interaction with the environment
(Thompson, Turner); the issuing of programmatic statements as
a kind of speech act (Caws, Juhasz/Ma); even the appropriation
of the spiritual technologies and iconography of occultism
and the mystical tradition (Bauduin, Morrison, Suárez). All
such practices provide ample openings for the elaboration of
a "Queer Surrealism." My focus in the foregoing analysis is,
certainly, to demonstrate the presence and relevance of the
phenomenological work done by such practices in defining or
creating specific identities, but also to unpack the productive
ways in which the practices interact to become a kind of "meta-
practice" animating a body of texts and their interpretations
which in turn flow back into lived experience becoming a kind
of *askesis* and creating both the narrative of a life and the life
thus narrated. In developing this notion I seek to tease out
the subtle relationship of experience and account; the way in
which what one says about one's self, whether to the world or
to one's self alone, becomes who one is. Thus I work to tease
out a conception of subjectivity as a process simultaneously
historical/textual and psychic. I endeavour to articulate
to some extent the ways in which being and doing are both

interdependent and self-conscious, which is to say both queer and surreal (in all senses of those words.)

We see the shape of such practice/praxis in what is left behind in the doing: books, artworks, films and so on. These products, the aesthetic traces of queer surrealist praxis, though complex and meaningful in and of themselves, are not and cannot be the *aims* of the praxis. As Don Lacoss memorably put it in relation to surrealism, "[t]he images, objects, and texts associated with Surrealism – let's say Meret Oppenheim's famous fur-lined teacup or Breton's bookl *Nadja* – are merely leftovers of a much more complicated process, the empty wine bottle on the table the morning after a satisfying evening of intense conversation or the footprints left behind in the snow after a passionate midnight dance under a dark sky" (viii). The art products of Queer Surrealism are not the goals, or the materialization of the actual horizon itself but exist as the material traces of the aesthetic aspirations to reach the horizon. Such traces are of great use and import in criticism as they can be used cartographically as one engages in a conceptual pursuit of the surreal and of queerness. They are a record of the work and a guide for moving it forward

While Lacoss, and Breton himself, were insistent that surrealism is not a literary (or artistic) movement, and gay liberation was conceived of as a political struggle, both movements have generated substantial bodies of work that are revelatory of the possibilities created by bringing them together in a Queer Surrealism. Moreover, though these *corpora* include both writing and other sorts of media, they situate both queerness and surrealism as practices of *scriptibility*, of reading and writing informed by eros, affect, and the notions of consciousness embodied in the esoteric tradition which, as Massicotte has demonstrated, provided the surrealists with "a model with which to unveil the limits and risks of subjectivity" (24). The deliberate cultivation of subjectivity by these means – conceived of, once again, as existing only in relationship to an *other,* are after all concretized or embodied through reading and writing both literally and figuratively.

In this way, I see Queer Surrealism as taking the "queer" half of its designation as not simply a noun nor a verb, but as implying both/neither at once, which is to say in a way entirely consistent with some of the expanded – and slippery – denotations already circulating among scholars (Eng *et al,* Halperin, Amin among them), artists and, increasingly, the general public as is evidenced by the growing circulation of terms like "heteroflexible." Moreover it takes surrealism too in its broadest sense, both as a series of particular theories and literary, artistic or existential techniques, and as an intuition or vision of *what will be* (a phrase used as the title of a recent surrealist anthology, pointedly enough)[92] whose rejection of the conditional "might" in its formulation underlines the speculative affirmation of potential at the heart of the surrealist project. Consistent with this, Queer Surrealism is meant as a place-holding term: one designating a zone of related meanings, of praxis and of potential. It is an object of study in this work and, at the same time, the methodology through which that object came into being. Moreover, the object itself

---

92 *What Will Be: Almanac of the International Surrealist Movement.* Bloemendaal: Brumes Blondes. 2014.

creates new knowledge and new forms of knowing. Queer Surrealism, if it is to be at all, will be not so much be an object or a school of thought as the articulation of a relationship; it will be a process, an action or series of actions, generated by and through a practice of subjectivity in dynamic relationship with the world. And it will be a highly mobile relationship at that. Techniques addressing eros, aesthesis, and the occult, and possibly others yet to be uncovered, will become central elements of a specific world-making and relational praxis that is perpetually repositioned and redefined against a fugitive utopian horizon.

The question of positionality evoked here echoes Sara Ahmed's work on queer phenomenology with its focus on how the subject's "orientation" arises from its relationship to space, the objects (in the very largest sense) in that space, and the extent to which they are familiar. She writes, "orientations involve different ways of registering the proximity of objects and others. Orientations shape not only how we inhabit space, but how we apprehend this world of shared inhabitance, as well as 'who' or 'what' we direct our energy and attention toward [sic]" (3). Such a phenomenological conception clearly relies upon a particular understanding of the relationship of mind and body in constructing an experiencing subject, both mind or "attention" and "intention" and the body being necessary for any comprehension of positionality; the haptic and visual senses are both engaged in the process. Moreover, Ahmed extends this insight into the delineation of a specifically "queer" phenomenology, stating that she too takes queerness "in at least two senses[...] First [....] as a way of describing what is 'oblique' or 'off line' [and] [s]econd,[...] to describe specific sexual practices" (161). The emphasis such statements lend to "obliqueness" or distance from the normative – and to the response to particular objects of interest, affection and attention (sexual and affectional[93] relations) implies that, for Ahmed, queer "orientation," which is to say the way in which queer minds and bodies operate in the world and respond to other objects/subjects, is active rather than "given". Queer orientation is *relational*, discernible as a matter of doing as well as being, and conceivable, primarily, as a question of praxis.

Nor can one undertake any serious reflection on how one orients oneself in the world without discussing language. It, too, is one of the foundational interfaces between the subject and the world, with speech or publication being powerful means of relating the content of consciousness to others, of *creating* a relationship. Marc Lafountain has written of surrealist praxis in a way that seems to speak directly to the queering of surrealism when he states that "[t]he erotic-sexual body is transfigured and confused with the erotic-textual body, resulting in a simulated eroticism whose meanings need to be considered now," (27). This identification of the sexual body with the textual body articulates the profound fluidity that exists between the relational subject and language that operates in and through him. Such fluidity – as I have argued above, in my second probe – is foundational for the movement. Moreover, the centrality of fluidity to praxis suggests it is equally

93 My use of this word here is certainly meant to denote relationships of "affection" in the ordinary dictionary sense, but I also welcome readings that take it in a broader way, as impinging on the realm of affect more generally.

foundational to the coherence of the subject in every way, which is to say as a particularly kinetic, formal articulation of the mind/body problem. As Julia Horncastle has noted regarding this experience in queerness specifically, "the body as a queer person lives and experiences it gives rise to the queer mind, which is neither cut off from nor separable from queer matter; that is, the queer body" (909). Horncastle offers a conception of the subject as continuous, connected to, and in relation with the world. The subject according to this formulation operates in the same ways Breton and Bataille, among others, describe it in their work: as an entity both complex and dynamic, but not divided.

Of course, the encounter of the subject and its literal and affective positionality with practices of writing, which is to say, *scriptibility* necessarily give rise to the question of how one conceives of and explains that subject, which is to say with the issue of *self-representation*. This has been the focus of much scholarly and artistic work over the last several decades and has led to significant changes in the conception of the mind-body complex, reformulations that are much driven by work in queer theory, and that are generating new ideas about the ways in which mind and body are, rather than binaristic and oppositional, co-constituting through their relationship. Most often these arguments turn traditional notions upside down, putting aside questions of ontology, what the body or the mind may be in and of itself – and foregrounding concerns with how they are constructed, shaped into specific kinds of people, particular kinds of subjects. Instead of positing static formulations of the subject, such models are invested in the phenomenon of becoming, in other words, in matters of process. Hardcastle suggests – in language resonant with the ideas of Ahmed and surrealism alike – that, given how the queer body/mind/subject is inevitably "othered," construed as in some ways oblique to the norm, it is "vital for queers to be able to articulate and validate (especially for themselves) their selfhood" (903). She asserts that this articulation of "queer being-ness [is] an orientation and a self-becoming." Hardcastle's claim is made manifest in many of the texts I have examined here, which are deliberate and self-aware representations of the subject in relation to the world and its processes, representational qualities that I have argued are Queer Surrealist.

To illustrate the generative force of the encounter of scriptibility and subjectivity in Queer Surrealist practice one may consider a number of case studies in which it takes on particular import. In an article in *The GLQ*, Anna Poletti examines life narratives, emblematic forms of self-representation, from the point of view of their performativity and periperformativity in a pertinent example of how recent queer theory has upended earlier accounts of subjectivity. Writing that a "life narrative is a performative utterance that brings into being both a life and a self [and reiterates] discourses and ideologies that constitute both personhood and the intelligibility of what meaning may be found in 'life' itself" (366), Poletti nonetheless complicates the well-established argument that such accounts "give voice" to marginalized groups. Instead, she favours a careful consideration of how narrative works on both formal and social levels, emphasizing the role of "collage" and "citation" in both their construction and reception: the ways in which such accounts might involve "the performance, close reading, and reenactment of popular culture in a way [that might] 'priz[e] the form away from its content' and valu[e] style and the 'playing of roles' "(Dyer, cited in Poletti, 370). Though Poletti here specifically points to the role of popular culture, the claim holds for any register of culture; Queer Surrealist deployments of esotericism are one form of citational praxis, for example. It is possible to view Carney's character in *The Real Thing*, who is profoundly concerned with shaping himself and gaining access to some form of transcendence through bondage and eroticized suffering, as doing precisely this. Moreover, the book's construction in epistolary form calls to mind Foucault's claims regarding the ways in which letters were a prominent feature of ascetic practices during the Classical period to the point that the self became a "theme or object (subject) of writing activity," (*Technologies*, 27), once more confirming scriptibiilty as central to Queer Surrealist praxis.

The precise dandyism of the bikers in Anger's *Scorpio Rising* provides further examples of the citational practice Poletti refers to, as does lppo Pohjola's documentary *Daddy & The Muscle Academy*. The latter film examines the impact of the erotic art of Tom of Finland (a figure who sometimes appears nearly ubiquitous in some quarters of post-war gay culture) on the subjectivity of contemporary gay leathermen. It is constructed in sections titled for Tom: "Tom's Name, "Tom's Technique," and "Tom's Influence" etc, each of which features a collage of images and interviews with the artist. These interviews are combined with testimony from the artist's admirers, a construction that lends his subcultural prominence far greater meaning. For example, interviews and shots of individual drawings and paintings are often intercut with sequences of both costumed and nude men in a setting suggestive of a sex club as they pose together in postures replicating some especially well-known Tom of Finland works. Voice-overs accompanying these sequences contain sexual vocalizations and repeated phrases such "I'm a Tom's Man" or "I'm one of Tom's men." Other intercut sequences feature men dressing in fetish outfits and working out, deliberately foregrounding the extent to which these men's identification with Tom's images led them to consciously shape their mind / attitude / personality and their body itself. Such sequences may be read in conjunction with the film's discussion of the work in terms of both its cultural role (Nayland Blake's references to an "invisible network" or the ways in which the drawings constitute "a blueprint for gay men's appearance in the late 20th century) and its impact on individuals, for example: one man's account of how he was told he had to look like the men he wanted and subsequently set out to transform himself. This format enlarges the film's effectiveness and highlights the extent to which certain kinds of identities are deliberate and self-consciously formulated: are a kind of askesis or self-fashioning. And, if Queer Surrealism is predicated on a cultivation of subjectivity via relationship, a deliberate structuring of the self in a desiring relation to the world is surely central to it.

Although the documentary is evidently non-fiction and Carney's book a novel, the former provides an account of how the *modus vivendi* of leathermen has developed into its present form and the latter documents, in ways that are verifiable from the historical record, how it emerged among men actively seeking to construct new ways of living. Thus, what joins the narratives of *The Real Thing* and *Daddy & The Muscle Academy* is the remarkable extent to which they both involve the account of a life or lives, or a way of living, which makes them "life narratives" in a loosely generic sense and consequently intriguing sites for research into subjectivity.

To provide more context for the notions of "self-fashioning" raised here, one must touch further on the work done in the area by Foucault. He famously spoke of ascesis, the care – or "technologies" – of the self "which permit individuals to effect [...] a certain number of operations on their own bodies and souls, thoughts, conduct, and way of being, so as to transform themselves in order to attain a certain state of happiness, purity, wisdom [etc.]" (*Technologies*, 18). Moreover he characterizes these practices elsewhere as being intended to "make the self appear" while proposing a "homosexual askesis that would make us work on ourselves and invent, I do not say discover, a manner of being that is still improbable." (*Live*, 309 - 310). Clearly, these men's donning of special garb, formalized sexual acts, and ritual embrace of danger can be viewed as work on the body and soul, but it is this emphasis on "invention" and the "improbable" that is most valuable to us as it stresses that it is *creative work*. Breton's major prose works clearly seek to generate improbable ways of being, or new kinds of awareness (the "supreme point" of the mind) in this way. They blend autobiographical incident with lyrical meditation and theoretical speculation in thoroughly "improbable" gestures:

Nadja concerns itself with his relationship to a woman and notions of madness seeking to tease out the connections and understand how they might change relationality; *Mad Love*, as has already been discussed, investigates the epistemological effects of romantic love and what is commonly called coincidence, positing psychic connections between them; and *Arcanum 17* blends myth and life and writing in complex ways. Moreover a similar analysis of *The Communicating Vessels* with its exploration of the relationship between waking life and dreams is possible. The impulse is clear among queer writers as well as we have seen in the manifestoes of Charles Shively, and in the analysis made here of *The Sexual Outlaw* – which documents Rechy's experiences of cruising and situates them in an explicitly political analysis – as a revolutionary practice.

Furthermore, such self-fashioning necessarily implies an approach to or movement towards some imagined ideal of the self, making it another iteration of Munõz's utopian horizon, always desired and always deferred, and when the work of self-fashioning intersects with the erotic as it does in the practices of leathermen, the transformative potential expands exponentially. The erotic as an attraction is, after all, always already both social and an urge to lose the self, to "shatter" it as Bersani notes.[94] Inherent in these deliberately constructed identities lies the fact that they are always embedded in a context of shared practice and never ultimately successful. They only exist in community; before people who recognize the ways in which they are constructed. In Anger and Carney's work this boundary play is highlighted; the will to both effort

94 See, in particular, his *Is the Rectum a Grave?*

and pleasure, to take subjectivity to its outer limits, to even the most extreme forms of *jouissance*, that intense pleasure Bataille describes as "assenting to life up to the point of death" (*Erotism*, 11)[95] and "[...] the blending and fusion of separate objects. It leads us to eternity, it leads us to death, and through death to continuity" (25)[96] is central. And that certainly suggests a model of the self in community that arguably steps past a place of either/or, of binaristic understandings of identity and the social, and toward one in which, as Tim Dean has noted "the shattering of the civilized ego betokens not the end of sociality but rather its inception" (*Antisocial*, 827).

MAKING: LOVE A POLITICS

In the end, such a structuring of Queer Surrealism must open up on the question of structures more broadly, which is to say the question of the political. The complexity of the utopian horizon underpinning Queer Surrealist praxis requires the conceptualization of the political in this analysis to be very broad; in this it follows the formulation of Bauduin *et al* in their assertion that "'politics' and 'political action' encompass not only strategies to affect material change within society, but any artistic tropes and strategies deployed to negotiate, question, deconstruct or rewrite discourses pertinent to issues of identity and individual transformation" (10). Both gay liberation and surrealism are concerned with personal transformation and political transformation; both take action on the level

95   "l'approbation de la vie jusque dans la mort," (*L'érotisme*, 17).
96   "à la confusion des objets distincts. Elle nous mène à l'éternité, elle nous mène à la mort, et par la mort, à la continuité [...]" (Ibid, 32).

of individual subjectivity and that of the collective sphere. Moreover, both self-consciously conceive of cultural or artistic work (writing, theatre, art, and so on) and political action as operating synergistically rather than divisively. Furthermore, in doing so, they create the richest possibilities for their respective programmes and lay the foundations for potential difficulties to arise. Thus, we must conceive of Queer Surrealism's politics not as isolated from literary, artistic and philosophical matters, but – because those interests are utopian in nature, and target an ideality, however elusive – as imbued with poetic and creative resonance that link it to emergent modes of political theorizing in the anarchist tradition.

This connection operates through the way "the utopian idea remains highly significant in contemporary anarchism [and] has to do with the ethos of prefigurative politics, or constructive direct action, through which anarchist utopian aspirations are transposed from the future to the present tense" (Gordon, 269), a temporal complexity that, to the extent it is embedded in a specifically affective and creative process, distinguishes it from simple historical revision and suggests the operation of something more complex. There are ways in which the surrealist conception of poetry is prefiguratively imbued with what John Moore, in another echo of surrealist thought, has called "Living Poetry," a politics that "is not merely interested in effecting changes in socioeconomic relations or dismantling the State, but in developing an entire art of living, which [is] simultaneously anti-authoritarian, anti-ideological and anti-political" (55) in which the last term is understood in relation to existing political arrangements. Thus, this complex play of temporality and meaning, of politics and prefiguration, postulates what anarchist theorist Clark has characterized as "the identity of means and ends" (20), and as our reflection thus far has focussed primarily on the latter half of Bauduin *et al*'s broad formulation, some brief consideration of the movements' politics in the more conventional sense is in order.

Much work on the politics of surrealism has focused on its relationship to Marxism and the French communist party, the Parti communiste français (PCF), in the 1930s. *The Politics of Surrealism* remains an important source for the movement's involvement in Marxist organizing and in its pages Helena Lewis outlines the extent to which the "Surrealists developed the most sustained and coherent political beliefs" (ix) of the modernist avant-gardes. Lewis traces the group's political development from the nihilism of the Dada years to their active engagement with the struggle against "war, nationalism, militarism, racism, colonialism and Christianity" (x) through to their years of activity with the PCF, in which their political commitment to revolution inevitably came into conflict with their ferocious instance on their autonomy as a group and as creators, particularly given the rise of doctrines of Socialist Realism during the 1930s. Their resistance to rigorous party discipline provoked a number of incidents within the membership and between them and party functionaries, notably the "affaire Aragon" which led to Louis Aragon's abandoning surrealism for communist activism. The crisis around the *Congrès international des écrivains pour la défense de la culture* (1935) is also noteworthy for its impact. In that incident, Breton's invitation to speak was withdrawn after he accosted, and slapped, Ilya Ehrenburg on the street and this may have, in turn, been a factor in Crevel's suicide (130-133).

Though the movement would make "tenacious efforts, set forth in some highly articulate polemical writing, to associate its intellectual, artistic, and moral preoccupations with the aims and methods of international communism" (Short, 3) there remained a streak of profound nonconformity and dedication to the furthest possibilities of life that would make accepting Party oversight extremely difficult for the surrealists. This conflict was undoubtedly rooted in the surrealist conception of revolution that required a change to life and the world at once; for them "[c]ommunism might represent a minimum programme, but it was the only force in existence capable of bringing about the social revolution which in turn was the necessary condition of 'une révolution dans les esprits'"(7). For surrealists, social and psychospiritual revolution were mutually dependent, consubstantial; the success of one required the other and the group faced an ongoing struggle to find some balancing point between them. Such a struggle is arguably in keeping with their larger project of finding a dynamic resolution for a whole range of perceived contradictions. That said, the involvement in and work with organized communism, despite often being characterized as by some writers as "brief" of "short-lived," would continue from about 1925 (when they publish the manifesto "*La Révolution d'abord et toujours !*") in *L'humanité*, the communist newspaper) until 1935 when Breton was deprived of his right to speak at the *Congrès*. The group's investment of a decade to political work of various kinds is the clearest possible testament to the seriousness of their commitment. And that commitment would not end with their departure from the party as is evidenced by Breton's collaboration with Trotsky on the *Fédération internationale de l'art révolutionnaire indépendant* (F.I.A.R.I.) (Lewis,146-150) and their activities and published tracts during the post-war years and since.

The divisions between the PCF and the surrealists ran deep and were rooted in foundational theoretical assumptions of which Breton was aware even as he attempted to position the surrealists among the leftists. Surrealism's dual focus lay at the heart of their troubles with orthodox communism; for them the revolutionary struggle was always both psychic, affective, and personal (the province of "life") and social, political, economic (that of "the world"), a divided loyalty that the party could, ultimately, never tolerate, particularly in the 30s. So central was this double revolution for the group that the painter Masson, once characterized surrealism, in another reference to the movement's the near-alchemical attempt to resolve contradictions, as "the collective experience of individualism" (cited in Short, 21).

The commitment to both individual and social liberation made a purely collectivist politics all but impossible for the surrealists, but it did create affinities with another political philosophy that has drawn recent scholarly attention: anarchism, which has always "run through Surrealists' political thought" (Löwy, 10). Breton acknowledges the significance of this affinity in his important postwar declaration "Tower of Light" which appeared in the anarchist journal *Le Libertaire*: "It is in the black mirror of anarchism that surrealism, long before it achieved self-definition, first recognized its own reflection" (264).[97] If some in the anarchist milieu were, like the communists, sceptical of surrealism due to its "complicity with 'hermeticism' and search for 'originality for originality's sake' endemic to modern art" (Cohn, 122) – an accusation founded in the misapprehension that surrealism saw itself primarily as an artistic movement – such pushback was less than that which they found in the organized communist left of the 1930s; moreover it did nothing to slow the cross-fertilization of surrealist and anarchist thinking in the 1950s, 1960s, and later. Of particular note in this regard is the work of Franklin and Penelope Rosemont who travelled to Paris in 1966 with the goal of meeting Breton (who welcomed them into surrealism shortly before his death) and subsequently established the Surrealist Movement in the United States in Chicago. The Rosemonts' surrealist publishing programme has since then included significant work on radical left politics (including the short-lived *Rebel Worker* journal and *Radical America*) thus "carving out a place for Surrealism in late twentieth-century anarchism" (Cornell, 251). Indeed, one must note of this ongoing intersection — as has Ron Sakolsky in his recent study – that anarchism has "been a formative and continuous leitmotif throughout the history of themovment" (8).

A close, and sometimes turbulent engagement with left politics has equally marked the trajectory of Gay Liberation. Jeffrey Escoffier summarizes the connection succinctly when he notes "[m]any early participants in the movements for

97 "Où le surréalisme s'est pour la première fois reconnu, bien avant de se définir à lui-même [...] c'est dans le miroir noir de l'anarchisme," (Claire Tour, 325)

lesbian, gay, bisexual, and transgendered people's rights had been involved in movements of the 1960s – the civil rights movement, the anti-war movement, the student movement, and the feminist movement" (41). This experience, unsurprisingly, meant that when queer people begin to organize in the wake of the Stonewall riots of June 1969 it was on a model liberally adapted from the counterculture and New Left. Toby Marotta's *The Politics of Homosexuality* suggests how crucial such experiences were in the immediate aftermath of the events:

> The crowds responsible for the street disorders that took place on several successive nights on Christopher Street [...] consisted largely of gay and straight hippies, Village residents and tourists. But they also included partisans of the New Left (like the reporters for Rat and the East Village Other) who saw an opportunity to stir homosexuals to join the Movement and homosexuals with countercultural views and values who had begun to think about their sexuality in the light of political perspectives popularized by the New Left. (76)

In this way, left politics were woven into the fabric of Gay Liberation at the very foundation, tying it to resistance to other forms of oppression, racial or gender for example, but also to a powerful critique of capitalism with echoes of some of the concerns of surrealism's "politics of eros." And, although these ideas often conflicted with more conservative gay activists and organizations, like the Mattachine Society, and would lead very quickly to the first schisms in the movement. Texts like historian John D'Emilio's essay "Capitalism and Gay Identity" demonstrate how these ideas persisted into the 1970s (and beyond). D'Emilio's article makes an especially pointed critique rooted in Marxist ideas of heterosexuality and the family as fundamental elements of a capitalist superstructure and suggests that gay liberation (as part of a larger sexual liberation) is necessary for meaningful social transformation – an idea clearly aligned with Shively's more imagistic radical writing. D'Emilio states: "[h]uman sexual desire need no longer be harnessed to reproductive imperatives, to procreation; its expression has increasingly entered the realm of choice. Lesbians and homosexuals most clearly embody the potential of this spirit, since our gay relationships stand entirely outside a procreative framework. The acceptance of our erotic choices ultimately depends on the degrees to which society is willing to affirm sexual expression as a form of play, positive and life-enhancing" (12). D'Emilio gave the talk on which his essay is based in the late 1970s originally, showing the continuity of New Left/Marxist influence on Gay Liberation after 1969 and, although the AIDS crisis would have a powerfully disruptive effect on the development of gay politics shortly after this period, this strain of left thinking has continued to have a (somewhat underground) influence on the movement through the present day, which remains detectable in the work of figures like Rubin or the *Against Equality Collective* and their interrogations of homonormative imperatives such as gay marriage or military service. Katz suggests something of the mechanics of this survival in his introduction to *The Gay Militants*, a documentary history of the year and half immediately following Stonewall when he points out that ACT UP activists in the 1980s would read the book in search of tips and techniques (xvi).

Moreover, and as with surrealism, proponents of Gay Liberation articulated even more radical positions informed by utopian and anarchist thought in addition to that of the mainstream Marxism. For our purposes here, and in our discussion of surrealism above, we use "anarchism" to denote, of course, the political philosophy and practice in its dictionary sense of pursuing a social arrangement without coercive governmentality but also in the subtler sense developed by the major anarchist thinkers. In the sense, for example, Goldman proposes when she writes: "[a]narchism, then, really stands for the liberation of the human mind from the dominion of religion; the liberation of the human body from the dominion of property; liberation from the shackles and restraint of government. Anarchism stands for a social order based on the free grouping of individuals for the purpose of producing real social wealth" (62) but also when she makes subtler claims like this: "[a]narchism is the only philosophy which brings to man the consciousness of himself; which maintains that God, the State, and society are non-existent, that their promises are null and void, since they can be fulfilled only through man's subordination. Anarchism is therefore the teacher of the unity of life; not merely in nature, but in man [sic]" (52). The sweeping claims made for sexual liberation and the dismantling of the traditional family and sex roles we see in manifestoes such as "Indiscriminate Promiscuity as an Act of Revolution" clearly reflect the influence of such anarchist thought among early gay liberationists, but the influence is generalized across the movement to a noteworthy extent both in its earliest days and more recently. Indeed, Gayle Rubin acknowledges this influence when she takes the title for her essay "The Traffic in Women" from the identically titled essay by Emma Goldman herself.

Dominic Ording's survey of early post-Stonewall texts brings us back to the synthetic function of a Queer Surrealism by bringing these traditions together through the suggestion, once again, of an alluring but fugitive utopian horizon. He makes the point that the utopian and anarchist impulses of the "recently liberated (at least ostensibly liberated) gay men attempted to articulate and embody new conceptualizations of intimacy, community, masculinity and gender roles and sexual politics, without the help of a any satisfactory existent models" (187) and quickly found that establishing "new identities as gay men with a sense of radical freedom as their main common rallying point proved difficult" (188). His observation is a reasonable one and the early Gay Liberationists did indeed face a number of issues in achieving a renewed politics and community, not the least of them being some divisions between activists themselves. The seriousness of this is noted by Shepard when he asserts that activists' visions of "freedom of the mind, body and spirit" (512) "could only take place when the Gay Liberation Front (GLF) rejected a Mattachine politics of respectability in favour of an anarchist impulse" (513). However, deeper issues were involved as well; in reviewing a range of early publications, by people like Paul Goodman and Konstantin Berlandt among others with this impulse in mind, Ording finds that the "[v]isions of utopias put forward in these

[197]

post-Stonewall texts were flawed: the aim was to determine a preconceived and highly prescriptive end rather that to see utopia as a process" (188). Queer Surrealism is imagined as one possible approach to help address – at least partly – that lapse, that failure to conceive of the project of liberation as a process, and one with no definite endpoint.

This sense of an endless quest for freedom, both psychic and social and political, is what marks our object here; this sense of an *atelic* adventure is what defines a Queer Surrealism: the perpetual setting out for a horizon that is at once always within our grasp – our shared grasp – and always inachievable. A horizon that combines Munõz's queerness and Breton's sublime point because in some ways they are one and the same; a conclusion made more visible by the number of concerns and techniques they share. Queer Surrealism finds its driving force and ontological basis in desire. The force of eros is what pulls it towards an utopian horizon because it makes it infinitely desirable. Aesthesis allows us to recognize and know that force of desire as it moves through the world, while one finds in the esoteric tradition a complex system for interacting with reality that is rooted in affect and the body. These three elements – eros, aesthesis and esotericism – severally and collectively constitute tools (though surely not the only ones) for moving towards the mobile horizon itself. Moreover, this trio, which was identified as operating in both traditions, replicates on the level of praxis, the central concern of a Queer Surrealism with *scriptibility*, moving from embodied perception to response to the attempt to have an effect on the world, to rewrite it, as it were, because all occult practices constitute attempts to shape reality in some way. And if the pursuit fails, one is at least doing something. Because Queer Surrealism *is* praxis: it is the pursuit itself. This may well be what underlies Foucault's identification of surrealism's discovery of "the domain of experience" (*André Breton*, 12), which points to an understanding of the movement's commitment to both knowledge and transformation coming together in experience.

Moreover, because Queer Surrealism is conceived of as a practice (or a praxis) both of writing and of life, and a practice done for its own sake, it is necessarily self-conscious. Queer Surrealism doesn't arise simply by recognizing the similarities between queer and surrealist practices of writing, it does so by bringing them together deliberately, knowingly, and with the intention of choosing not simply to engage in both, but to foreground their shared overlaps, to make visible what might otherwise have been simply implicit. It stresses the subject as scriptible – as formed, as shaped, indeed *written* – *and* as defined by relationality, in relationship with the utopian horizon it pursues, certainly, but with everything else it might encounter along the way: the body, the unconscious, other people, unexpected objects, in short the world. Queer Surrealism acknowledges that the subject does not exist outside these relationships and is consequently never complete, never arrived at any more than one arrives at the beckoning utopian horizon.

Queer Surrealism is comfortable with failure. Not only does it accept failure, it embraces it, knowing that failure prompts us back to movement once again, back to the pursuit. And Queer Surrealism knows that such pursuit is one thing open to us, one hope for something *more* and that is in itself is a kind of success. Because, whether one achieves the horizon or not, its pursuit – the cultivation of experience, the embracing of community – prefigures it, and allows at least some sense of liberty, some loving contact; it offers at last, some imagined and affective experience of the horizon even as it flickers and, in the words of Clark once more, "[e]ven if it can never be attained utopia is already present or it is a fraud" (21). This presence is prefigurative in the way so much of the political practice of anarchism has been over the course of the last century, because its endpoint too is utopian, and offers no certainty. It too "represents" as Graeber writes " a certain ideal – in its purest form probably unattainable. It is a form of action in which means and ends become, effectively, indistinguishable: a way of actively engaging with the world to bring about change, in which the form of the action [...] Is itself a model for the change one wishes to bring about" (210). In this it is a companion to Walter Benjamin's backward gazing angel of history, one that appears, recast, in Breton's vision of another angel:

The angel of Liberty, born from a white feather shed by Lucifer during his fall, penetrates the darkness; the star she wears on her forehead grows larger, becomes "first meteor, then comet and furnace." We see how where it may once have been unclear, the image sharpens: it's rebellion itself, rebellion alone is the creator of light. And this light can only be known by way of three paths: poetry, liberty, and love, which should inspire the same zeal and converge to form the very cup of eternal youth, at the least explored and most illuminable spot in the human heart. (*Arcanum 17*, 97)[98]

Breton's angel looks not behind her, but resolutely forward. And though Breton calls her the angel of liberty, she is also the angel of utopia. Her gaze is ever fixed on the horizon, the furthest limit, should such a thing exist; she looks neither up nor down, but always directly towards the furthest point. The place where sky and sea meet and where a misty light, neither that of dusk nor that of dawn, congeals in the space of their union, filled with the suggestion of astounding things taking form, new things congealing and coming into the world. Strange possibilities. The angel knows she is both chasing and being pulled towards it, acting and acted upon at once: another strange possibility, another new thing.

Her wings carry her high above the surface of the world, and in her flight she follows the planet's curve, so that even as she rushes forward, a falcon stooping on some moving prey, she begins anew because she has necessarily crossed a point passed many times before. And she knows that the world too is moving, and so she is always late, her arrival impossibly deferred. Despite this impossibility, she goes on, partly, one must acknowledge, for the view, which is always marvellous, always beautiful, but mostly because her flight is a kind of embrace; it is a way of loving an always moving world.

98   "L'ange Liberté, née d'une plume blanche échappée à Lucifer durant sa chute, pénètre dans les ténèbres; l'étoile qu'elle porte à son front grandit, devient 'météore d'abord, puis comète et fournaise.' On voit comme, en ce qu'elle pouvait encore avoir d'incertain, l'image se précise: c'est la révolte même, la révolte seule qui est créatrice de lumière. Et cette lumière ne peut se connaître que par trois voies: la poésie, la liberté et l'amour qui doivent inspirer le même zèle et converger, à en faire la coupe même de la jeunesse éternelle, sur le point moins découvert et le plus illuminable du coeur humain," (*Arcane 17*, 121)

WORKS CITED

PRIMARY SOURCES (TEXT)

Louis Aragon. (1924). *A Wave of Dreams*. London: Thin Man Press. 2010.

Une vague de rêves. Paris: Éditions Seghers. 2006.

Georges Bataille. *The Absence of Myth: Writings on Surrealism*. (Michael Richardson, trans and ed) London: Verso. 1994.

———— *Erotism: Death and Sensuality*. (1957). Mary Dalwood, (trans.) San Francisco: City Lights Books. 1986.

L'érotisme. Paris: Les éditions de minuit: Collection Arguments. 2004.

———— *Inner Experience*. (1943). Albany: State University of New York Press. 1988.

L'expérience intérieure, Paris: Éditions Gallimard, Collection Tel. 2009.

———— "Madame Edwarda". (1941). *My Mother. Madame Edwarda. The Deadman*. London: Marion Boyars.1989. "Madame Edwarda." *Romans et Récits*. Paris: Gallimard, Pléiade. 2004.

———— "On the Subject of Slumbers." (1946) Georges Bataille. *The Absence of Myth: Writings on Surrealism*. Michael Richardson, (trans and ed.) London: Verso. 1994.

"À propos d'assoupissements." *Oeuvres Complètes: XI, Articles 1*. Paris: NRF/ Gallimard. 1988.

———— *The Sacred Conspiracy: The Internal Papers of the Secret Society of Acéphale and Lectures to the College of Sociology*. (Additional Texts by Roger Caillois, Pierre Klossowksi, Michel Leiris. *et al.*) Maria Alletti and Alastair Brotchie (eds.) London: Atlas Press. 2017.

———— *Story of the Eye*. (1928). San Francisco: City Lights Books. 1987 .

"Histoire de l'oeil." *Romans et Récits*. Paris: Gallimard, Pléiade. 2004.

———— "The Surrealist Religion." (1948) Georges Bataille. *The Absence of Myth: Writings on Surrealism*. Michael Richardson, (trans and ed.) London: Verso. 1994.

"La religion surréaliste." *Oeuvres Complètes: VII*. Paris: NRF/ Gallimard. 2009.

Charles Baudelaire. *Paris Spleen: Little Poems in Prose*. Middletown: Wesleyan UP. (Keith Waldrop, trans.) 2009.

"Petits Poèmes en prose (Le Spleen de Paris.)" *Oeuvres Complètes*, Paris: Seuil, l'Intégrale. 1968.

André Breton. *Arcanum 17*. (1945) Toronto: Coach House Press. Zack Rogow, trans. 1994. *Arcane 17, Enté d'Ajours*. Paris: 10/18. 1970.

————"Ascendant Sign," (1947). *Free Rein*. Lincoln: University of Nebraska Press. 1995.

"Signe ascendant." *La clé des champs*. Paris: Jean-Jacques Pauvert. 1967.

———— *Conversations: The Autobiography of Surrealism*. (1952). (Trans. Mark Polizzotti.) New York: Marlowe & Company. 1993.

————"Crisis of the Object." (1936). *Surrealism and Painting*. (Simon Watson Taylor, trans.) Boston: MFA Publications. 2002.

"Crise de l'objet." *Le surréalisme et la peinture*. Paris: Gallimard. 1979.

———— "Free Union." *Poems of André Breton: A Bilingual Anthology*. Jean-Pierre Cauvin and Mary Ann Caws (eds and trans.) Austin: University of Texas Press. 1982.

"L'Union libre." *Poems of André Breton: A Bilingual Anthology*. Jean-Pierre Cauvin and Mary Ann Caws (eds and trans.) Austin: University of Texas Press. 1982.

————"A Letter to Seers" (1925). *Manifestoes of Surrealism*. Ann Arbor: University of Michigan Press. 1981.

"Lettre aux voyantes". *La Révolution Surréaliste: Collection Complète*. Paris: Jean- Michel Place. 1975.

———— *Mad Love*. (1937). Mary Ann Caws. (trans.) Lincoln: University of Nebraska Press. 1987.

L'amour fou. Paris: Gallimard: Collection Folio. 2003.

———— "The Marseilless Deck," (1953). *Free Rein*. Lincoln: University of Nebraska Press. 1995.

"Le jeu de Marseilles." *La clé des champs*. Paris: Jean-Jacques Pauvert. 1967.

———— "The Mediums Enter." (1922). *The Lost Steps*. Lincoln: University of Nebraska Press.1996.

"Entrée des médiums." *Les Pas Perdus.* Paris: Gallimard, Collection Soleil. 1969. —— "Pierre Molinier" (1956). *Surrealism and Painting.* Simon Watson Taylor. (trans.) Boston: MFA Publications. 2002.

"Pierre Molinier." *Le surréalisme et la peinture.* Paris: Gallimard. 1979. —— "Soluble Fish" (1924). *Manifestoes of Surrealism.* Ann Arbor: University of Michigan Press. 1981.

Poisson soluble. Paris: Gallimard: Collection Poésie. 1996.

—— "Speech to the Congress of Writers." (1935). *Manifestoes of Surrealism.* Richard Seaver & Helen R. Lane. (trans.) Ann Arbor: University of Michigan Press. 1981. "Discours au Congrès des Ecrivains." *Position Politique du Surréalisme.* Paris: Denoël Gonthier, Bibliothèque Médiations. 1972.

——-"Surrealist Exhibition of Objects." (1936). *Surrealism and Painting.* Boston: MFA Publications. 2002.

"Exposition surréaliste d'objets." *Le surréalisme et la peinture.* Paris: Gallimard. 1979.

——-"The Surrealist Manifesto." (1924). *Manifestoes of Surrealism.* Ann Arbor: University of Michigan Press. 1981.

"Manifeste du surréalisme." *Manifestes du surréalisme.* Paris: Gallimard, folio essais. 2000.

—— "Second Manifesto of Surrealism." (1930). *Manifestoes of Surrealism.* Ann Arbor: University of Michigan Press. 1981.

"Second manifeste du surréalisme." *Manifestes du surréalisme.* Paris: Gallimard, folio essais. 2000.

—— "Surrealist Situation of the Object." (1935). *Manifestoes of Surrealism.* Ann Arbor: University of Michigan Press. 1981.

"Situation surréaliste de l'objet." *Position Politique du Surréalisme.* Paris: Denoël Gonthier, Bibliothèque Médiations. 1972.

——-"Tower of Light." (1952) *Free Rein.* Lincoln: University of Nebraska Press. 1995.

"La claire tour." La Clé des Champs. Paris: Jean-Jacques Pauvert. 1967.

—— "What is Surrealism?" (1934). *What is Surrealism?: Selected Writings.* Franklin Rosemont (ed.) New York: Monad Press. 1978.

Qu'est-ce que le surréalisme? Paris: Actual. 1986

André Breton, Philippe Soupault. *The Magnetic Fields.* (1920).

London: Atlas Press. 1985.

Les Champs Magétiques. Paris: NRF, Gallimard. 1976.

André Breton et al. The "Manifesto on l'Age D'Or," in Breton, *What is Surrealism:*

Selected Writings. Franklin Rosemont. (ed.) Monad Press, New York, 1978,

André Breton et al., "Manifeste des surréalistes à propos de l'Âge d'or", *L'avant-scène. Cinéma,* 27-28 (15 juin - 15 juillet 1963). Paris: Cinémathèque. p. 24-27.

———— "The Declaration of January 27, 1925." (1925). Maurice Nadeau. *The History of Surrealism.* Cambridge: Belknap Press of Harvard University Press. 1989

"Déclaration du 27 janvier 1925." *Histoire du surréalisme, suivi de documents surréalistes.* Paris: Éditions du seuil. 1964.

Ronnie Burk. *Sky*Boat.* Oakland: Kolourmeim Press, 2011

William Carney. *The Real Thing.* (1968). New York: Richard Kasak Books. 1995.

Ithell Colquhoun. *The Goose of Hermogenes.* London: Peter Owen. 2003.

Steven Dansky, John Knoebel, and Kenneth Pitchford. "The Effeminist Manifesto." *We are Everywhere: A Historical Sourcebook of Gay and Lesbian Politics.* Mark Blasius, Shane Phelan. Eds. New York: Routledge. 1997.

Samuel R. Delany. *The Motion of Light on the Water: Sex and Science Fiction in the East*

Village, 1957 - 1965. New York: New American Library. 1988.

Arthur Evans. *Witchcraft and the Gay Counterculture.* Boston:Fag Rag Books. 1978.

———— *The God of Ecstasy: Sex-Roles and the Madness of Dionysos.* New York: St. Martin's Press. 1988.

Charles Henri Ford and Parker Tyler. *The Young and Evil.* (1933). New York : Richard Kasak Books. 1996.

Jack Fritscher."Corporal in Charge of Taking Care of Captain O'Malley." *Gay Roots: Twenty years of Gay Sunshine.* (Winston Leyland, Ed). San Francisco: Gay

Sunshine Press. 1991. ———— *Some Dance to Remember.* Stamford: Knight's Press. 1990.

Emma Goldman. *Anarchism and Other Essays.* New York: Dover

Publications. 1969.

Harry Hay. *Radically Gay.* Will Roscoe. (ed.) Boston: Beacon Press. 1996.

Jack Kerouac. "Essentials of Spontaneous Prose." (1953). June 11, 2017. http://www.writing.upenn.edu/~afilreis/88/kerouac-spontaneous.html

Winston Leyland, Ed. *Gay Roots: Twenty years of Gay Sunshine.* San Francisco: Gay Sunshine Press. 1991.

John Rechy. *The Sexual Outlaw.* New York: Dell Publishing.1977.

——— *City of Night.* New York: Grove Press. 1963.

Penelope Rosemont (ed.) *Surrealist Women: An International Anthology.* Austin: University of Texas Press. 1998.

Kurt Seligmann. *The Mirror of Magic: A History of Magic in the Western World* (1948). Collector's edition. Rochester, Vermont: Inner Traditions. 2018.

Charles Shively. "Indiscriminate Promiscuity as an Act of Revolution." *Gay Roots: Twenty Years of Gay Sunshine.* Winston Leyland. (ed.). San Francisco: Gay Sunshine Press.1991.

Carl Wittman. "A Gay Manifesto." *Come Out Fighting: A Century of Essential Writing on Gay & Lesbian Liberation.* Chris Bull (Ed). New York: Thunder's Mouth Press/Nation Books. 2001.

PRIMARY SOURCES (FILM/VIDEO)

Blueboys. (1976). Dir. N/A. Perf. Peter Berlin, Marc Majors. 20 minutes. Included on *Nights in Black Leather* Gorilla Factory Productions. U.S. A. 2007. DVD.

Daddy and the Muscle Factory. (1991). Dir. Ilppo Pohjola. Perf. Tom of Finland, Durk Dehner. Zeitgeist Video. 1993. U.S.A. 55 minutes. DVD.

Nights in Black Leather (1973). Dir. Ignatio Rutkowski. Perf. Peter Berlin, Rick Jedin, Al Joffrey, Jeff Salum,Tom Webb. Gorilla Factory Productions. U.S. A. 99 minutes. 2007. DVD.

Pornography: A Thriller. Dir. David Kittredge. Perf. Matthew Montgomery, Pete Scherer, Jared Grey. Wolfe Video. 2014. U.S.A. 113 minutes. DVD. *That Man: Peter Berlin.* Dir. Jim Tushinski. Perf. Peter Berlin, Armistead Maupin, John Waters. Gorilla Factory Productions. 2005. U.S. A. 81 minutes. DVD.

That Obscure Object of Desire. Dir. Luis Buñuel. Perf. Fernando Rey, Carole Bouquet, Ángela Molina. The Criterion Collection. 2001. France/Spain. 102 minutes. DVD.
Scorpio Rising. (1963). Dir. Kenneth Anger. Fantoma. 2007. DVD.
Waldeslust. (1973). Dir.n/a. Perf. Peter Berlin and unknown. 10 minutes. Included on *Nights in Black Leather* .Gorilla Factory Productions. U.S. A. 2007. DVD.

SECONDARY SOURCES

Carl Abrahamsson. "The Deconstruction of a Map of an Unknown Territory."in Genesis Breyer P-Orridge. *The Psychick Bible: Thee Apocryphal Scriptures of Genesis Breyer P-Orridge*. Port Townsend: Ferhal House. 2006.
Elza Adamowicz. *Surrealist Collage in Text and Image: Dissecting the Exquisite Corpse*. Cambridge: Cambridge University Press. 1998.
Dawn Ades, Michael Richardson, Krzysztof Fijalkowski (eds.) *The Surrealism Reader: An Anthology of Ideas*. London: Tate Publishing. 2016.
Margot Adler. *Drawing Down the Moon: Witches, Druids, Goddess-Worshippers, and Other Pagans in America Today (Revised and Expanded Edition)*. Boston: Beacon Press. 1986.
Sara Ahmed. *Queer Phenomenology: Orientations, Objects, Others*. Durham: Duke University Press. 2006.
Juan Vicente Aliaga. "Jambe, Mollet, Pied, Anus… Je Vous Aime." *Infernal Metamorphosis: The Life and Art of Pierre Molinier*. Candice Black (ed.) London: Creation Books/Wet Angel. 2009.
Richard D. Altick. *Victorian People and Ideas: A Companion for the Modern Reader of Victorian Literature*. New York: W. W. Norton and Co. 1973.
Kadji Amin "Haunted by the1990s: Queer Theory's Affective Histories." *WSQ: Women's Studies Quarterly*. 44: 3 & 4 (Fall/Winter 2016). 179-189.
David Arnold. *Poetry and Language Writing: Objective and Surreal*. Liverpool: Liverpool University Press. 2007.
Kevin Arnold. "Male and Male and Male: John Rechy and the Scene of Representation." *Arizona Quarterly: A Journal of American Literature, Culture, and Theory*. Spring 2011. 67 (1). 115-134.

Wayne Baerwaldt. "Pierre Molinier." *Pierre Molinier*. Alison Gillmor, Wayne Baerwaldt. (eds.) Winnipeg: Plug In Editions. 1993.

Anna Balakian. *Surrealism: The Road to the Absolute*. Chicago: University of Chicago Press. 1986.

Tessel M. Bauduin. *Surrealism and the Occult*. Amsterdam: Amsterdam University Press. 2014.

Tessel M. Bauduin, Victoria Ferentinou, and Daniel Zamani (eds). *Surrealism, Occultism and Politics: In Search of the Marvellous*. London: Routledge. 2018.

Tom Beckett. "Interview with CA Conrad." *E-X-C-H-A-N-G-E-V-A-L-U-E-S*. August 2006. Web. http://willtoexchange.blogspot.ca/2006/08/interview-with-caconrad.html

Robert Bellin. "Retrospection and Prophecy in the Structure of 'Mad Love.'" *Journal of Modern Literature*. 30 (2) Winter, 2007. 1 - 16.

Leo Bersani. *Is the Rectum a Grave and Other Essays*. Chicago: The University of Chicago Press. 2010.

Manuel Betancourt. "Cruising and Screening John: John Rechy's *The Sexual Outlaw*, Documentary Form and Gay Politics." *GLQ: A Journal of Lesbian and Gay Studies*. 2017. 23(1).

Donald H. Bishop. *Mysticism and the Mystical Experience: East and West*. Mississauga: Associated University Presses. 1995.

Maurice Blanchot. *The Infinite Conversation*. (trans. and with an introduction by Susan Hanson.) Minneapolis: University of Minnesota Press. 1993.

Boyz magazine. Thursday, August 19 2010. Page 18. London: Swallow Digital Services Ltd. Michael Cabanatuan. "Ronnie Burk - Dissident AIDS Activist." San Francisco Gate. (Tuesday, March 25, 2003).

http://www.sfgate.com/news/article/Ronnie-Burk-dissident-AIDS-activist-2660390.php

Garrett Caples, Andrew Joron, Nancy Joyce Peters. "High Poet: The Life and Work of Philip Lamantia." *The Collected Poems of Philip Lamantia*. Caples, Joron and Peters (eds.) Berkeley: University of California Press. 2013.

Caruth, Cathy. *Unclaimed Experience: Trauma, Narrative, and History*. Baltimore: Johns Hopkins University Press, 1996.

Mary Ann Caws. *Manifesto: A Century of Isms*. Lincoln: University of Nebraska Press. 2001.

Jacqueline Chénieux-Gendron. "Toward a New Definition of
    Automatism: *L'immaculée Conception.*" *André Breton Today.* Anna
    Balakian and Rudolf E. Kuenzli (eds). New York: Willis Locker
    & Owens. 1989.
John P Clark. "Anarchy and the Dialectic of Utopia." *Anarchism and
    Utopianism.* Laurence Davis and Ruth Kinna (eds.) Manchester:
    Manchester University Press. 2009.
Margaret Cohen. *Profane Illumination: Walter Benjamin and the Paris
    of Surrealist Revolution.* Berkeley: University of California Press.
    1993.
Jesse Cohn. *Underground Passages: Anarchist Resistance Culture 1848 -
    2011.* Oakland: AK Press. 2014.
Ingrid Beytrison Comina. "André Breton's Studio, or the
    Magnetism of Objects". *Surrealism and Non-Western Art: A
    Family Resemblance.* Berlin: Hatje Cantz/ Fondation Pierre
    Arnaud. 2014.
Katharine Conley. *Automatic Woman: The Representation of Woman in
    Surrealism.* Lincoln: University of Nebraska University Press.
    1996.
———— "Sleeping Gods in Surrealist Collections." *Symposium.* Vol.
    67. No. 1. 2013. 6 - 24.
———— "Surrealism and Outsider Art: From 'The Automatic
    Message" to André Breton's Collection." *Yale French Studies:
    Surrealism and its Others.* No. 109. 2006. 129 - 143.
———— "Surrealism's Ghostly Automatic Body." *Contemporary
    French and Francophone Studies.* 15 (3). June, 2011. 297 - 304.
Randy P. Conner. *Blossom of Bone: Reclaiming the Connections between
    Homoeroticism and the Sacred.* New York: Harper SanFrancisco.
    1993.
Peter Tracey Connor. *Georges Bataille and the Mysticism of Sin.*
    Baltimore: The Johns Hopkins University Press. 2000.
Andrew Cornell. *Unruly Equality: U.S. Anarchism in the 20th Century.*
    Oakland: University of California Press. 2016.
Drew Daniel. "Trading Futures: Queer Theory's Anti-Anti-
    Relational Turn." *Criticism.* 52.2 (Spring 2010). 325 - 330.
C. B. Daring, J. Rogue, Deric Shannon, Abbey Volcano (eds.)
    Queering Anarchism: Addressing   and Undressing Power and Desire.
    Oakland: AK Press. 2012.

Laurence Davis and Ruth Kinna (eds.) *Anarchism and Utopianism*. Manchester: Manchester University Press. 2009.

Tim Dean. "The Antisocial Homosexual" in "The Antisocial Thesis in Queer Theory." *PMLA*. Vol. 121. No. 3 (May, 2006), pp. 819-828.

—— *Beyond Sexuality*. Chicago: Univesity of Chicago Press. 2000.

—— *Unlimited Intimacy: Reflections on the Subculture of Barebacking*. Chicago: University of Chicago Press. 2009.

—— "Sam Steward's Pornography: Archive, Index, Trace." *Samuel Steward and the Pursuit of the Erotic*. Debra A. Moddelmog and Martin Joseph Ponce (eds.) Columbus: The Ohio State University Press. 2017.

John D'Emilio. "Capitalism and Gay Identity." (1983). *Making Trouble: Essays on Gay History, Politics, and the University*. London: Routledge. 2013.

Martin Duberman. *Has the Gay Movement Failed?* Oakland: University of California Press. 2018.

Lisa Duggan and José Esteban Muñoz. "Hope and hopelessness: A dialogue." *Women & Performance: a journal of feminist theory*. 19 (2). July 2009. 275-283.

Rachel Blau DuPlessis and Peter Quartermain. *The Objectivist Nexus: Essays in Cultural Poetics*. Tuscaloosa: University of Alabama Press. 1999.

Jonathan P. Eburne. *Surrealism and the Art of Crime*. Ithaca: Cornell University Press. 2008.

Friedrich-Wilhelm Eickhoff. "On *Nachträglichkeit*: The modernity of an old concept." *International Journal of Psychoanalysis*. 87:6 (December 2006). 1453 - 1469.

—— "Nachträglichkeit from the perspective of the phylogenetic factor in Freud's 'Moses and Monotheism.'" *The Scandinavian Psychoanalytic Review*. 29:1 (2006). 53 - 59.

Richard Ellmann. *Oscar Wilde*. New York: Alfred A. Knopf. 1988.

David L. Eng, Judith Halberstam, and José Esteban Muñoz. "Introduction: What's Queer About Queer Studies Now." *Social Text*. 84-85 (Vol. 23, Nos. 3-4). Fall-Winter 2005.1-17.

Jeffrey Escoffier. "Emancipation, Sexual Liberation, and Identity Politics." *New Politics*. 12: 1. (Summer 2008). 38-43.

Brett Farmer. *Spectacular Passions: Cinema, Fantasy, Gay Male*

Spectatorships. Durham: Duke University Press. 2000.

Victoria Ferentinou. "Surrealism, Occulture and Gender: Women Artists, Power and Occultism." *ARIES* 13 (2013). 103 - 130.

Patrick Ffrench. *The Cut: Reading Bataille's Histoire de l'oeil*. Oxford: Oxford University Press.1999.

Krzysztof Fijalkowksi. "Convulsive Beauty." *Surrealism: Key Concepts*. Michael Richardson and Krzysztof Fijalkowksi (eds.) London: Routledge. 2016.

Haim Finkelstein. "Breton and Dalí - The Utopian Eros in Exile." *L'Esprit Créateur*. 36 (4), 76-86.

Michel Foucault. "André Breton: a Literature of Knowledge." *Foucault Live: Collected Interviews, 1961 - 1984*. New York: Semiotext(e). 1989.

———— "Sex, Power, and the Politics of Identity." *Foucault Live: Collected Interviews, 1961 - 1984*. New York: Semiotext(e). 1989.

———— "Technologies of the Self." *Technologies of the Self: A Seminar with Michel Foucault*. Gutman, Hutton and Martin (eds.) Amherst: The University of Massachusetts Press. 1988.

Elizabeth Freeman. "Introduction." *GLQ: A Journal of Gay and Lesbian Studies*. Vol 12. 2-3. (*Queer Temporalities*). 2007. 159 - 176.

Sigmund Freud. *The Freud Reader*. Peter Gay. (ed.) New York: W. W. Norton & Co. 1989.

———— *Introductory Lectures on PsychoAnalysis*. (1917). Pantianos Classics. n.d. 1990. ———— *New Introductory Lectures on Psycho-Analysis*. (1933). New York: W. W. Norton & Co. 1990.

———— "*Project for a Scientific Psychology*" in Standard Edition, Volume 1, 283 - 397.

———— *Standard Edition of the Complete Psychological Works of Sigmund Freud*. James Strachey, editor and translator. London: Hogarth, 1953 -1974.

Philip Gefter. *Wagstaff: Before and After Mapplethrope: A Biography*. New York: Liveright. 2014.

Jerome Gellman. "Mysticism." *The Stanford Encyclopedia of Philosophy*, (Spring 2017 Edition). Edward N. Zalta (ed.) https://plato.stanford.edu/archives/spr2017/entries/mysticism/

James Gifford. "Late Modernism's Migrations: San Francisco Renaissance, Egyptian anarchists, and English Post-Surrealism"

Textual Practice. 29 (6). 1051 - 1075.

Uri Gordon. "Utopia in Contemporary Anarchism." *Anarchism and Utopianism.* Laurence Davis and Ruth Kinna (eds.) Manchester: Manchester University Press. 2009.

Peter Gorsen. "The Artist's Desiring Gaze on Objects of Fetishism." *Pierre Molinier.* Alison Gillmor, Wayne Baerwaldt. (eds.) Winnipeg: Plug In Editions. 1993.

David Graeber. *Direct Action: An Ethnography.* Oakland: AK Press. 2009.

David M. Halperin. *Saint Foucault: Towards a Gay Hagiography*, New York: Oxford University Press. 1995.

Corie J Hammers. "The Queer Logics of Sex/Desire and the 'Missing' Discourse of Gender." Sexualities. 2015. Vol. 18 (7). 838-858.

Byung-Chul Han. *The Agony of Eros.* Erik Butler. (trans.) Cambridgeshire: MIT Press. 2017.

Oliver Harris. "Cutting Up the Corpse." *The Exquisite Corpse: Chance and Collaboration in Surrealism's Parlor Game.* Kanta Kochhar-Lindgren, Davis Schneiderman, and Tom Denlinger (eds.) Lincoln: University of Nebraska University Press. 2009.

Steven Harris. *Surrealist Art and Thought in the 1930s: Art, Politics, and the Psyche.* Cambridge: Cambridge University Press. 2004.

Colin Herd. "Present Tense: CA Conrad's While Standing in Line for Death." *3:AM Magazine.* (October 12, 2017). http://www.3ammagazine.com/3am/present-tense-caconrads-standing-line-death/

Inés Hernández-Ávila. "Ronnie Burk." *Chicano Writers: Third Series.* Francisco A. Lomeli and Carl R. Shirley. (eds.) Detroit: Gale, *Dictionary of Literary Biography Vol. 209.* 1999. (Literature Resource Center, go.galegroup.com/ps/i.do?).

Mark Hewson and Marcus Coelen. "Introduction." Hewson and Coelen. (eds.) *Georges Bataille: Key Concepts.* London: Routledge. 2016.

Lucas Hilderbrand. "Historical Fantasies: 1970 Gay Male Pornography in the Archives." *Porno Chic and the Sex Wars: Amercian Sexual Representation in the 1970s.* (Carolyn Bornstein and Whitney Strub. (eds.) Amherst: University of Massachusetts Press. 2016.

Jess Byron Hollenback. *Mysticism: Experience, Response, and Empowerment.* University Park: Pennsylvania State University Press. 1996.

Julia Horncastle. "Queer Orientation: Selfhood and Poetics." *Continuum: Journal of Media and Cultural Studies.* 23 (6). December, 2009. 903-920.

Alexander Howard. "Camp, Modernism, and Charles Henri Ford." *Modernism/ Modernity.* 23 (1). 2016. 9 - 13.

John Hoyles. "Bataille and Surrealist Pornography: Dance or Treadmill?" *Journal of European Studies.* 1995. 25 (1). 51-66.

Heather Duerre Humann. "Nachträglichkeit and 'Narrative Time' in Jennifer Egan's *A Visit from the Goon Squad.*" *Pennsylvania Literary Journal.* 9: 2. (Summer 2017). 85-97.

Brian Jackson. "Modernist Looking: Surreal Impressions in the Poetry of Allen Ginsberg." *Texas Studies in Literature and Language.* Vol. 52 (3). Fall 2010. 298 - 323.

Andrew Joron. *Neo-Surrealism or The Sun at Night: Transformations of Surrealism in American Poetry 1966-1999.* Oakland: Kolourmeim Press. 2010.

Alexandra Juhasz and Ming-Yuen S. Ma. "Introduction. Queer Media Manifestoes." *GLQ: A Journal of Lesbian and Gay Studies.* 19.4. (2013): 560-561.

Just Out: Oregon's Gay/Lesbian/Bi/Trans newsmagazine. September 18, 2009. Page 33.

Raihan Kadri,with Michael Richardson and Krzysztof Fijalkowksi. "Objective Chance." *Surrealism: Key Concepts.* Michael Richardson and Krzysztof Fijalkowksi (eds.) London: Routledge. 2016.

Jonathan Ned Katz. "Introduction to the 1995 Edition." *The Gay Militants: How Gay Liberation Began in America, 1969 - 1971.* Donn Teal. New York: St. Martin's Press. 1995.

Andreas Kilcher. "Seven Epistemological Theses on Esotericism: Upon the Occasion of the 10th Anniversary of the Amsterdam Chair." *Hermes in the Academy: Ten Years' Study of Western Esotericism at the University of Amsterdam.* Wouter J. Hanegraaff dan Joyce Pijnenburg (eds.). Amsterdam: Amsterdam University Press. 2009.

Nina Kokkinen. "Occulture as an Analytical Tool in the Study of

Art." *ARIES* 13 (2013). 7 - 36.

Bruce LaBruce. "What I Said to Peter Berlin und Vhat Hee Sat to Mee." *Porn Diaries.* Herzogenrath: Editions Moustache. 2016.

Jacques Lacan. *Écrits.* New York: W. W. Norton & Company. 2006.

——— *The Four Fundamental Concepts of Psychoanalysis.:The Seminar of Jacques Lacan Book XI.* New York: W. W. Norton & Company. 1998.

Donald Lacoss. "Introduction: Surrealism and Romantic Anticapitalism." *Morning Star: Surrealism, Marxism, Anarchism, Situationism, Utopia.* Michael Löwy. (Austin: University of Texas Press. 2009.

Marc Lafountain. "Bataille's Eroticism, Now: from Transgression to Insidious Sorcery." *Philosophy and Desire.* Hugh Silverman (ed.) New York: Routledge. 2000.

Jean Laplanche & Jean-Bertrand Pontalis. *The Language of Psychoanalysis.* (1973). Karnac. 2006.

John Lauritsen. Gay Liberation in New York: Year One. *Gay and Lesbian Review Worldwide.* July-August 2009. 27 - 29.

Patricia Leavy. *Method Meets Art: Arts-Based Research Practice.* The Guildford Press. 2009.

Helena Lewis. *The Politics of Surrealism.* New York: Paragon House. 1988.

David Lomas. *The Haunted Self: Surrealism, Psychoanalysis, Subjectivity.* New Haven: Yale University Press. 2000.

Heather Love. "Queer Theory's Everything Problem" cited in Kadji Amin "Haunted by the 1990s: Queer Theory's Affective Histories." *WSQ: Women's Studies Quarterly.* 44: 3 & 4 (Fall/Winter 2016). 173 - 189.

Natalie S. Loveless. "Towards a Manifesto on Research - Creation." *RACAR: revue d'art candienne/Canadian Art Review.* 40:1. (2015). 52 - 54.

Michael Löwy. *Morning Star: Surrealism, Marxism, Anarchism, Situationism, Utopia.* Austin: University of Texas Press. 2009.

Alyce Mahon. *Surrealism and the Politics of Eros 1938 – 1968.* New York: Thames & Hudson. 2005.

Steven Marcus. "Marx's masterpiece at 150." *The New York Times.* 26 April 1998.

Consulted June 13, 2016.

Toby Marotta. *The Politics of Homosexuality: How Lesbians and Gay Men have made themselves a Political and Social Force in Modern America*. Boston: Houghton Mifflin Company. 1981.

Claudie Massicotte. "Spiritual Surrealists: Séances, Automatism and the Creative Unconscious." *Surrealism, Occultism and Politics: In Search of the Marvellous*. Tessel M. Bauduin, Victoria Ferentinou and Daniel Zamani eds. London: Routledge. 2018.

J.H. Matthews. *Toward the Poetics of Surrealism*. Syracuse: Syracuse University Press. 1976.

Rollan McCleary. *A Special Illumination: Authority, Inspiration and Heresy in Gay Spirituality*. London: Equinox Publishing. 2004.

Janine Mileaf. "Body to Politics: Surrealist Exhibition of the Tribal and the Modern at the Anti-Imperialist Exhibition and the Galerie Charles Ratton." *RES: Anthropology and Aesthetics*. No. 40 (Autumn, 2001). 239-255. John Moore. "Lived Poetry: Stirner, anarchy, subjectivity and the art of living." *Changing Anarchism: Anarchist Theory and Practice in a Global Age*. Jonathan Purkis and James Bowen (eds.). Manchester: Manchester University Press. 2004.

Patrick Moore. *Beyond Shame: Reclaiming the Abandoned History of Radical Gay Sexuality*. Boston: Beacon Press. 2004.

Mark Morrison. "Ethel Colquhoun and Occult Surrealism in Mid-Twentieth Century Britain and Ireland." *Modernism/modernity*. Volume 21, No. 3, September 2014, 587-616

Jennifer Mundy. "Letters of Desire." *Surrealism. : Desire Unbound*. Princeton: Princeton University Press, 2001.

Jennifer Mundy (ed.) *Surrealism : Desire Unbound*. Princeton: Princeton University Press, 2001.

José Esteban Muñoz. *Cruising Utopia: The Then and There of Queer Futurity*. New York: New York University Press. 2009.

———— "Ephemera as Evidence: Introductory Notes to Queer Acts." *Women & Performance: a journal of feminist theory. Volume* 8, No. 2, 5-16.

———— " 'Gimme Gimme This… Gimme Gimme That': Annihilation and Innovation in the Punk Rock Commons. *Social Text* 31.3. (2013). 95 - 110.

Eileen Myles. "Afterword."*The Book of Frank*. (CA Conrad.) Seattle & New York: Wave Books. 2009.

Judith Noble. "The Light Behind the Lens: The Occult Cinema of Kenneth Anger." *Abraxas, Special Issue 2: Luminous Screen*. London: Fulgur Esoterica. 2014.

Dominic Ording. "Intimate Fellows: Utopia and Chaos in the Early Post-Stonewall Gay Liberation Manifestoes." *Anarchism and Utopianism*. Laurence Davis and Ruth Kinna (eds.) Manchester: Manchester University Press. 2009.

Christopher Partridge. *The Re-Enchantment of the West. Volume 1*. London: T & T Clark International. 2004.

Octavio Paz. *Alternating Current*. New York: Arcade Publishing. 1967.

Charles Sanders Peirce. "What is a Sign?" *The Essential Peirce: Selected Philosophical Writings, Volume 2 (1893 - 1913)*. Peirce Edition Project. (eds.) Bloomington: Indiana University Press. 1998.

Jose Pierre. *Investigating Sex: Surrealist Researches 1928-1932*. Malcolm Imrie. (trans.) London and New York: Verso. 1992.

Anna Poletti. "Periperformative Life Narrative: Queer Collages." *GLQ: A Journal of Lesbian and Gay Studies*. 22:3, 2016. 359 - 379.

Mark Polizzotti. *Revolution of the Mind: The Life of André Breton*. New York: Farrar, Straus and Giroux.1995.

Gerhard Poppenberg. "Inner Experience" *Georges Bataille: Key Concepts*. Hewson and Coelen. (eds.) London: Routledge. 2016.

Anna Powell. 'The Occult: A Torch for Lucifer." *Moonchild: The Films of Kenneth Anger*. Jack Hunter (ed.) London: Creation Books. 2001.

Jean-Michel Rabaté. *The Cambridge Introduction to Literature and Psychoanalysis*. New York: Cambridge University Press. 2014.

Michael Richardson. "Introduction." Georges Bataille. *The Absence of Myth: Writings on Surrealism*. Michael Richardson, (trans and ed.) London: Verso. 1994.

Andrew Ridker. "Queer Bubbles: How CA Conrad Turns Ritual Into Poetry." *The Paris Review*. (July 6, 2017). https://www.theparisreview.org/blog/2017/07/06/queer-bubbles/

Bill Rodgers. "The Radical Faerie Movement: A Queer Spirit Pathway." *Social Alternatives* Vol. 14, No. 4 (October 1995). 34-37.

Gayle Rubin. "Thinking Sex." *Deviations: A Gayle Rubin Reader*. Durham: Duke University Press. 2011.

———— "The Traffic in Women." *Deviations: A Gayle Rubin Reader.* Durham: Duke University Press. 2011.

Christina Helena Rudosky, "André Breton the Collector: A Surrealist Poetics of the Object" (2015). University of Colorado, Boulder: PhD Dissertation. *French & Italian Graduate Theses & Dissertations.* 6. http://scholar.colorado.edu/frit_gradetds/6

Charles Rycroft. *A Critical Dictionary of Psychoanalysis.* New York: Penguin Books. 1995.

Ron Sakolsky. *Dreams of Anarchy and the Anarchy of Dreams: Adventures at the Crossroads of Anarchy and Surrealism.* . New York: Autonomedia. 2021.

Madan Sarup. *An Introductory Guide to Post-Structuralism and Postmodernism.* Athens: University of Georgia Press. 1989.

Peter Savastano. "Gay Men as Virtuosi of the Holy Art of Bricolage and as Tricksters of the Sacred." *Theology & Sexuality.* 14.1. 9-28.

Eve Kosofsky Sedgwick. *Touching Feeling: Affect, Pedagogy, Performativity.* Durham: Duke University Press. 2003.

———— "Queer and Now." *Tendencies.* Durham: Duke University Press. 1993.

Sam See. "Making Modernism New: Queer Mythology in The Young and the Evil." *ELH* 76. 2009. 10073 - 1105.

Benjamin Shepard. "Bridging the Divide Between Queer Theory and Anarchism." *Sexualities.* 13:4. (2010). 511 - 527.

Michael Sheringham. "Breton and the Language of Automatism: Alterity, Allegory, Desire." *Surrealism and Language.* Ian Higgins (ed.) Edinburgh: Scottish Academic Press. 1986.

Robert Short. "The Politics of Surrealism, 1920 - 36." *Journal of Contemporary History.* 1:2. (1966). 3 - 25.

Hugh J. Silverman. "Introduction: Twentieth Century Desire and the Histories of Philosophy." *Philosophy and Desire.* Hugh Silverman (ed.) New York: Routledge. 2000.

Katja Silverman. *The Threshold of the Visual World.* New York: Routledge. 1996.

Peter Sloterdijk. *You Must Change Your Life: On Anthropotechics.* Cambridge: Polity Press. 2013.

Justin Spring. *Secret Historian: The Life and Times of Samuel Steward, Professor, Tattoo Artist, and Sexual Renegade.* New York: Farrar, Straus and Giroux. 2010.

Kirsten Strom. *Making History: Surrealism and the Invention of a Political Culture.* Lanham: University Press of America. 2002.

Juan A Suárez. *Bike Boys, Drag Queens, and Superstars.* Bloomington: Indiana University Press. 1996.

Michael Székely. "Text, trembling: Bataille, Breton and surrealist eroticism." *Textual Practice* 19(1), 2005, 113–129.

Michael S. Sherry. *Gay Artists in Modern American Culture: An Imagined Conspiracy.* Chapel Hill: The University of North Carolina Press. 2007.

Allan Stoekl. "Recognition in Madame Edwarda." *Bataille: Writing the Sacred.* London: Routledge.1995.

Rachel Leah Thompson. "The Automatic Hand." *Invisible Culture.* No. 7. Spring, 2004. 1-18

Hugh B. Urban. *Magia Sexualis: Sex, Magic, and Liberation in Modern Western Esotericism.* Berkeley: University of California Press. 2006.

Amos Vogel. *Film as a Subversive Art.* New York: Random House. 1974.

Scott Watson. "Pierre Molinier: Natural Historian." *Pierre Molinier.* Alison Gillmor, Wayne Baerwaldt. (eds.) Winnipeg: Plug In Editions. 1993.

Barrett Watten. *The Constructivist Moment: From Material Text to Cultural Poetics.* Middletown: Wesleyan University Press. 2003.

Thomas Waugh. *Hard to Imagine: Gay Male Eroticism in Photography and Film from their Beginnings to Stonewall.* New York: Columbia University Press. 1996. ——— "The Third Body: Patterns in the Construction of the Subject in Gay Male Narrative Film." *Queer Looks: Perspectives on Lesbian and Gay Film and Video.* Gever, Greyson and Parmar. (eds.) Toronto: Between the Lines. 1993.

Linda Williams. *Figures of Desire: A Theory and analysis of Surrealist Film.* Berkeley: University of California Press. 1981.

Willy (pseudonym of Henry Gauthier-Villars). *The Third Sex.* (1927) Lawrence R.Schehr. (trans. and intro.) Chicago: University of Illinois Press. 2007.

Carl Wittman. "A Gay Manifesto." *Come Out Fighting: A Century of Essential Writing on Gay & Lesbian Liberation.* Chris Bull (ed). New York: Thunder's Mouth Press/Nation Books. 2001.

Peter Dubé holds a PhD in the humanities from Concordia University's Centre for Interdisciplinary Studies in Society and Culture (CISSC), and is a multi-genre writer, translator, and independent scholar.

He is the author, co-author or editor of a dozen books of fiction, non-fiction and poetry. His novella, *Subtle Bodies*, an imagined life of French surrealist René Crevel was a finalist for the Shirley Jackson Award, and his most recent work, a novel in prose poems entitled *The Headless Man*, was shortlisted for both the A. M. Klein Prize and the ReLit award. He was a member of the editorial committee of the contemporary art magazine *Espace*, art actuel for 18 years and is currently co-editor of The *Philosophical Egg*, an organ of living surrealism. He lives and works in his hometown of Montreal.

www.ingramcontent.com/pod-product-compliance
Lightning Source LLC
Chambersburg PA
CBHW072047190526

45165CB00019B/1995